John C. Cusick and Katherine F. DeVries

THE
BASIC
GUIDE TO
YOUNG
ADULT
MINISTRY

ORBIS BOOKS

Maryknoll, New York 10545

Founded in 1970, Orbis Books endeavors to publish works that enlighten the mind, nourish the spirit, and challenge the conscience. The publishing arm of the Maryknoll Fathers and Brothers, Orbis seeks to explore the global dimensions of the Christian faith and mission, to invite dialogue with diverse cultures and religious traditions, and to serve the cause of reconciliation and peace. The books published reflect the views of their authors and do not represent the official position of the Society. To learn more about Maryknoll and Orbis Books, please visit our website at www.maryknoll.com.

Library of Congress Cataloging-in-Publication Data

Cusick, John C.
    The basic guide to young adult ministry / John C. Cusick and Katherine F. DeVries.
      p. cm.
    Includes bibliographical references and index.
    ISBN 1-57075-392-X (pbk.)
    1. Church work with young adults – United States. 2. Young adults – Religious
life – United States. 3. Catholic Church – United States – Membership. I. DeVries,
Katherine F. II. Title.

BX2347.8.Y64 C87 2001
259′.25 – dc21

                                       2001034605

THE
BASIC
GUIDE *To*
YOUNG
ADULT
MINISTRY

To
Rev. Patrick H. O'Neill,
the Father of Young Adult Ministry
in the American Catholic Church

Contents

Foreword

Church officials do not often resort to secular terms for vocabulary to describe the church's ministerial activity. The language of the marketplace brings with it a wide variety of connotations that often do not serve the religious context within which we work. The opposite is also true. The secular world often finds religious language deficient or heavily burdened with connotations that do not fit the world of supply and demand. In many respects, however, young adults are very comfortable speaking and understanding both secular and religious language. And those who minister to young adults must be aware of the cross-fertilization those young adults bring from their workaday world into the experience and practice of their faith.

John Cusick and Katherine DeVries have written a commonsense book on *marketing the Catholic Church for young adults.* The church has always been engaged in the field of marketing—perhaps without ever using that specific word and always for a much loftier goal than mere profit. Young adults are a distinct and important segment of the market that the church must attract. This book is a helpful as well as a hopeful resource for carrying out that important task more effectively. The authors have achieved remarkable success in young adult ministry in the Archdiocese of Chicago and as consultative and resource personnel for many other dioceses during the past two decades. This book is a compilation of their approach, their successes, and their design. It represents both strategies that they have found to work with young adults as well as recommendations that might avoid likely disappointments for ministers as well as young adult Catholics.

The book is basic and practical. It offers wisdom that is time tested and that the authors have found to be enduring. Above all, it attempts to acquaint potential as well as experienced young adult ministers with issues and needs that John and Kate have found to be present among most of the young adults with whom they have worked.

The book draws upon the best within the Catholic Church's tradition of evangelization and mission, and it combines that with sound sociological, personal developmental, and marketing theories. The result is a fascinating description of how the church ought to reach out to and successfully engage a vitally important segment of its people.

This is a practical pastoral resource. It does not pretend to offer a theology of working with or serving young adult Catholics; it simply describes what the authors have found to be advantageous in their ministry. John Cusick and Kate DeVries have established an enviable reputation as successful servants of young adult Catholics. This book shares what they have learned in working with and serving young adults.

The book also clearly hints at what has made John and Kate so successful. They love young adults and draw support for their own life of faith in and through their encounters with young adult Catholics. The book will not teach you how to find faith-energy from young adults, but its deepest wisdom will never be accessible unless you somehow discover what Kate and John have obviously found to be true and to be a great source of hope for them and those for whom they care so ardently.

†Wilton D. Gregory

Bishop of Belleville

Preface

Young adults, people in their twenties and thirties, married and single, have become the most elusive part of the Catholic population. Every bishop, every pastor, every leader of church organizations wants to reach them. When asked, "Where are your younger members?" some shake their heads and say that few younger people seem to be interested. Many parish and Catholic organization leaders, after failing to attract young adults, seem paralyzed as to how to engage young adults in Catholic Church life. All agree that without them, the life of the church will quickly diminish. Before we know it, today's young adults will be tomorrow's middle-aged leaders. What would the church be like without them?

This book says there is nothing to fear. *There is a way.*

In *Sons and Daughters of the Light,* their pastoral plan for ministry with young adults, the National Conference of Catholic Bishops identified four goals for an effective outreach to young adults:

- connecting young adults with Jesus Christ
- connecting young adults with the church
- connecting young adults with the mission of the church in the world
- connecting young adults with a peer community.*

The Basic Guide to Young Adult Ministry offers strategies for accomplishing each of these goals.

Within these pages you'll find a practical, pastoral approach for inviting women and men in their twenties and thirties, married and single, into greater participation in the life of the church. It is the fruit of the experience of more than two decades that the Young Adult Ministry Office for the Archdiocese of Chicago has been in existence. It is the product

---

*National Conference of Catholic Bishops, *Sons and Daughters of the Light: A Pastoral Plan for Ministry with Young Adults* (Washington, D.C.: United States Catholic Conference, 1997), 28–41.

of thousands of ideas and hundreds of pilot projects, which have touched tens of thousands of lives. It is also the realization of the dream of what can happen when good people gather in the Lord's name. We invite you to enter into that dream, specifically as it relates to young adults.

This guide is intended for the following groups of people:

1. Bishops, pastors, associate pastors, pastoral associates, and parish administrators who seek to pass on the faith to the young adult generation.

2. Directors of religious education, directors of adult formation programs, directors of RCIA (Rite of Christian Initiation of Adults), and directors of young adult ministry programs who are responsible for gathering this segment of the adult population, but who would greatly appreciate some help, fresh ideas, and practical, affordable suggestions to make that happen.

3. Diocesan leaders responsible for Family Life, Catechesis, Catholic Education, Ministry in Higher Education, Evangelization, Minority Concerns, Marriage Preparation, Justice Ministry, Ecumenism, Respect Life, Parish Councils, and any other office who are entrusted with the privilege of inviting young adults into their organizations.

4. Leaders with vision—paid professionals as well as generous volunteers—who have a passion for this age group and see the value in the presence and active participation of young adults in the Catholic Church.

5. Young adults themselves who want to gather with their peers and become more involved in their church, but are not sure how to begin.

6. Leaders of parish groups and church organizations who want to "regenerate" their group or organization with the presence of young adults.

7. Missionary societies and congregations interested in attracting a new generation to their unique charisms.

8. People of all denominations and faiths who want to do more with and for young adults.

9. Anyone wishing to learn more about a ministry to this talented, faith-filled group of people on an occasional or regular basis.

If you are interested in regenerating your diocese, parish, or organization with the vital presence of people in their twenties and thirties, you have obtained a resource that has already proven fruitful. You can read this guide from beginning to end, or you can jump to the sections that interest you most and will be the most beneficial to you.

Part One looks at who young adults are, their affiliation with the Catholic Church, what they seek, and why a ministry directed specifically to them makes sense.

Part Two presents information about effective young adult ministry at the parish level.

Part Three discusses young adult ministry beyond the parish—both as an areawide outreach in which several parishes combine resources and as a diocesan outreach. This section also contains specific information about the work of the Young Adult Ministry Office for the Archdiocese of Chicago, including ways of recruiting and using volunteers effectively. Since its inception in 1977, this office has

- developed a mailing list that has gone from twenty names and addresses in 1978 to twenty-eight thousand in 2001;

- published a quarterly newsletter, sent to the entire mailing list;

- begun a monthly e-letter, e-mailed to over two thousand young adults;

- managed the growth of the Theology-on-Tap program from one host parish in 1981 to sixty-five host parishes in the Chicago area today;

- celebrated an annual Mass and picnic with the archbishop of Chicago—as a conclusion to Theology-on-Tap. Over fourteen hundred young adults attend the Mass in Holy Name Cathedral with the cardinal presiding. Approximately twelve hundred stay for a picnic with the cardinal on the lawn of his residence;

- created one of the largest one-day gatherings of young adults in the country—the annual FOCUS conference;

- produced a variety of programs responding to the needs of young adults: Transitions—A Day to Explore Movements in Your Work Life; Relationships! What a Trip! Catholicism Revisited—Perhaps It's That Time in Your Life to Re-examine Your Religious Roots; P.S.—Prayer & Scripture; We Are More Than We Seem—A Day to Explore Spirituality for Men; Pearls of Wisdom—A Day to Explore Spirituality for

Women; Rest-a-Little Weekend Retreat; YACHT Club (Young Adult Catholics Hanging Together); You're As Good As You Feel—A Look at Healthy Living; and Volunteers-in-Action;

- initiated a number of special interest groups: Small Faith Communities; Divorced/Separated Support Groups; Dialogue Groups; Young Married Couples Groups; Jewish/Catholic Couples Dialogue Group; Adult Children of Alcoholics (ACOA) Groups; Grief Support Group;

- gathered young adults for the "First Sunday Mass" on the first Sunday of every month at 11:15 all year long, every month of every year since 1984;

- offered annual leadership training to parish leaders;

- created a website: www.yamchicago.org.

It is our sincere wish that this material helps you to better understand young adults and that you encourage and invite them into fuller participation in the life of the church. If as a result of this material women and men in their twenties and thirties feel that they are more welcome in their church, that their gifts are appreciated, and that the church has quality worship, programs, and activities for them, we will have achieved our purpose.

PART ONE

THE CURRENT STATE OF AFFAIRS

Chapter 1

Look Who's Missing
and See Who's There

In the not too distant past, the backbone of Catholic Church life, from parishes and organizations to ordained and professed religious, was people twenty-five to forty-five years old. On most levels of the church today, the leadership is still held by that same group—not the same age group, but the same people now twenty to thirty years older.

A quick nonscientific look at who is involved supports that statement. Sadly, much of traditional Catholic organizational life has aged with the organizations themselves—from Holy Name Societies to Serra Clubs, St. Vincent de Paul Societies to the Legion of Mary. Consider those Catholic organizations of which you are aware. What is the average age of their members? What is the age of their leaders? Who seems to be missing? Here is some data on current leadership of our parishes: The average age of diocesan priests in active ministry in the United States is fifty-nine; that of religious priests is sixty-three. As of 1998, the median age of all religious sisters was sixty-eight. The average age of lay ministers currently is fifty, brought down primarily by the presence of youth ministers, 57 percent of whom are under the age of forty.* Additionally, publishers tell us that most subscribers and readers of Catholic magazines and many diocesan newspapers are over the age of sixty.

Ask priests and lay people to take a survey of who is involved in parish councils, liturgical ministries, the Christian Family Movement, and Renew groups, and who attends weekend Masses. The answer all too often is families with school-aged children and senior citizens.

---

*Bryan T. Froehle and Mary L. Gautier, *Catholicism USA: A Portrait of the Catholic Church in the United States* (Maryknoll, N.Y.: Orbis Books, 2000).

In spite of these statistics, there is some hopeful and positive news about our Catholic population. When questioned about their religious affiliation, people say that they *like* being Catholic. Catholics continue to affiliate with the church at the same rate they did thirty years ago. The one exception is Catholics who remarry outside the Catholic Church after divorce. According to data gathered by Michael Hout, sociology professor at the University of California, "Between 17 and 20 percent of Catholics who have divorced and subsequently remarried leave the church in connection with their remarriage. Although some of them leave organized religion altogether, most of them join Protestant congregations and become active and contributing parishioners."* Young adults, however, are not leaving the church for something else. Unfortunately, that comforting fact does not help us to pay the bills, or fill our pews, convents, rectories, and church organizations.

Although some would claim that "young adults are not around any longer," that is simply not true. Though many parishes seem older than ever before, young adults are the ones getting married, are having their children baptized, and are heavily invested as participants in the RCIA program. They are also seen at wakes, funerals, weddings, and first holy communion and confirmation services. They connect at times of great joy and times of great pain. They are around, but if attendance was taken on any given Sunday, for the most part we would mark the young adult age group "absent."

The data reveal an interesting finding. There is a widening gap between affiliate Catholics (those who, when asked, say they are Catholic but do not attend church regularly) and practicing Catholics. Thirty years ago a good, practicing Catholic was one who went to church weekly. Today regular church attendance is defined as two to three times a month. That is a significant change. Yet in many Catholic parishes, business as usual continues.

Let's face it. To some degree, we have become a local church focused on teaching our children and "saving the saved." Of course caring for our children is a high priority and should always be so. But what happens when those children become adults, and many, for whatever reasons, become

*Michael Hout, "Alienation among Divorced and Remarried Catholics in the United States," *America*, December 16, 2000, 10–12.

Evangelization and catechesis in young adult ministry

Evangelization means presenting the vision and tradition of our faith and inviting others to experience faith. Evangelization will be a strong component in a ministry to young adults. After all, women and men in their twenties and thirties are the largest segment of the Catholic population, and they are the least active part of that same population.

Catechesis means presenting the teaching and wisdom of the Catholic faith through programs, spiritual activities, sacramental moments, and conferences. Catechizing young adults often means assisting them to move from the faith they learned as children to a personal appropriation of the faith as adults.

less active or inactive in the church? This is a serious question that is demanding our attention on a number of levels, including the financial level. How much longer can we keep asking the same (though fewer) church-going activists for more of their money and time? More importantly, can we honestly continue to call ourselves the Body of Christ when so many members are regularly missing and we are not actively encouraging their presence?

A reflection on young adults and their relationship to the church might lead us to get serious about the church's mission of evangelization and catechesis. The first step is to define a target group for that mission. A look at who is involved and not involved, who is present and not present will quickly reveal that a good place to begin is with our own people, primarily those in their twenties and thirties. We call them "young adults."

The term "young adult" was not in vogue several generations ago. The twenties and thirties did not appear to be young. People married soon after completing school and were parents by the age of twenty-five. The adjective "young" didn't appear to matter. They were adults—earning a living and raising a family as participating members in church, schools, government, and social communities. Some young adults were "veterans" of foreign wars before they had even turned thirty.

As Gail Sheehy accurately describes it in her book *New Passages*, today

Demographics

More than 40 percent of all adult Catholics in the U.S. today are young adults, aged eighteen to thirty-nine. They are the largest segment of the Catholic population.

many of the twenty-somethings are living a prolonged adolescence. They are staying in school longer, are delaying their marriages, and are less certain about job and career paths. And now, with job loyalty a mere textbook concept, they will change jobs or careers five or six times before their early retirement.

Relationship to church is different, too. Traditionally, contact with the Catholic Church, besides Sunday Mass, was at the time of sacraments. After baptism came confession and holy communion. Those moments were followed by confirmation and then marriage, and the cycle repeated itself with the next generation. One young man we know commented that he is living in the "time between sacraments"—between confirmation and (he hopes) marriage. That time is longer now than it has ever been. If it wasn't the sacramental moments that brought young adults into closer contact with the parish church, it was their progeny—the formation and education of the next generation. You became involved for the sake of the kids. Not only are they marrying later, but some couples are also choosing to wait before having children. As more time passes between sacramental moments, the traditional reasons for being connected to a faith community seem to fade. The high rate of marriage breakup clouds this picture even more.

The following statements about this age group are typical:

Young adults are just not interested in the Catholic Church. They do not attend Sunday Mass regularly, and they don't support the parish.

Once they get married, you don't see them again. The same thing applies to the baptism of their children. Once the water has been poured, they stay away until it is time for religious instruction in five or six years.

When the parents of young adults gather, they often share stories of just how few of their kids go to church any longer.

A young adult retreat is a wonderful way to feed spiritual hunger and generate community. Here young adults celebrate Eucharist to conclude a very successful retreat.

Secular and religious literature today reveals a good news/bad news scenario about which we need to be concerned. That literature indicates that there is a deep spiritual hunger expressed by many Americans. It is a hunger for meaning, definition, and direction in life. It is rooted in questions about what really matters. It reaches higher than career goals, as important as those can be, to seek a purpose in one's life more fundamental than work or social status. Yet those same searchers and seekers acknowledge that they are having a hard time getting their spiritual hunger satisfied in institutional churches. How can that be? Isn't the church the place to find the sacred and spiritual—*the* table at which to be fed?

There are, however, an enormous number of young adults who have had good church experiences through high school and college campus ministry programs. Those experiences and programs feed thousands of spiritually hungry people every year.

Knowing that today's young adults still affiliate with the Catholic Church at a consistent rate and that there is a great spiritual hunger among them might be the glimmer of hope that is needed. They are not leaving the Catholic Church in droves. For many young adults, calling themselves Catholic appears to be enough. Also, many do practice their Catholic faith, but in nonconventional forms that are not always consistent, visible, or measurable.

Church has a great deal to offer those who get involved and stay connected. But consider that there might not be a lot to attach oneself to if you are not a senior citizen or the parent of a school-aged child. Interestingly, as important as both of these groups are, in a great many parishes even combined they form a minority. A clear majority of people within some parish boundaries are rightly concerned that there is little that addresses their needs.

If we are serious about the church's mission of evangelization and catechesis, and if we and some carefully chosen others accept the challenge of making our own young adults the target group of our efforts, then we must go at it a different way. Instead of being paralyzed by the situation that exists, we can use it as a springboard to *what can be*. Jesus was a person of great dreams. He saw possibility. So can we.

Young adults are not an indifferent, consumer-driven, narcissistic group who care little for what the church is or does. They are our people. They keep telling us so. They are God's people. They are not the future of the church. They are the present church waiting to be welcomed. We have much to offer; they have much to learn. They have much to give; we have much to receive.

Church and young adults should be an easy fit. They tell us they are spiritually hungry; we have the Bread of Life. They are altruistic; we have many opportunities for them to serve the world in Jesus' name. They are searching for meaningful relationships and people with whom to share life; our parishes and organizations are filled with great and wonderful people—the Body of Christ.

Please consider the following questions. Mull them over in your mind or write down your responses on a piece of paper. You'll be beginning your own young adult ministry program here and now!

- Who are your young adults?

- For what are they searching?

- What insights did you come away with from conversations you have had with young adults?

- What have they revealed to you about the world in which they live, their needs, their fears, and their hopes?

- What have they said to you about the church in general and your parish or organization in particular? What one activity or event might make a difference to them?

Effective church ministry is built upon listening to and learning from the actual lived experiences of people. If you had trouble answering any of these questions, consider gathering some young adults and having a conversation with them about what they would find helpful.

Chapter 2

Regenerating Catholicism

It is time that our church, in all its dimensions—parishes, agencies, and organizations—becomes pro-active in our outreach to our own younger people. We have already mentioned that young adults continue to be Catholic, but counting their warm bodies is not enough. The strategy is to reach out, invite, welcome, and actively enlist their time, energy, talent, and altruism. If we keep using the word "evangelization," then let's be realistic and honest about who most needs to be evangelized—our own Catholic people.

As a church, we don't seem to understand that point at all. The single largest group who are not active in our Catholic system are not former Catholics. They are today's affiliative Catholics, and many of them are young adults. Calling yourself Catholic is one thing; doing something about it is another.

Consider the following reflection by one pastor: "Our Sunday afternoon Mass attracts lots of younger Catholics. Those involved in the parish, several handfuls, sit up front. But the majority sit along the outside of the side aisle pews and in the very back of the church. While presiding at Mass, I can also see more people standing in the back and looking around to see if they recognize anyone. We have got to find a way for them to move from the side to the center and then up to the front." Amen.

Our Catholic faith is a great treasure and a gift to the world. It offers people a marvelous means of transforming the world into the image of God. As a church, in spite of all that has happened to us and to American society in the last several decades, we have a low conversion rate in comparison to mainline Christian denominations. And as mentioned previously, we have maintained one of the most consistent affiliation rates for the same amount of time.

Do we have the talent, the drive, and, most especially, the attitude needed to welcome and respond to our own young adults? That concern was spoken loudly and clearly by young adults whose opinions we invited. A twenty-five-year-old woman observed:

One thing that any successful outreach by parishes to young adults is going to have to address is the fact that not only are many priests unprepared to deal with us, but many parishioners are as bad or worse. Not only do they not understand young adults, they do not want to. Unless the parish leadership, not just the priests, are prepared to make a parish welcoming to young adults, all efforts are doomed to fail. Please listen to us; most parishes not only do not understand young adults, they do not want to.

In our dealings with the growing number of affiliative Catholics, we need missionary zeal, not judicial inquiry. We need to learn, some of us for the first time, how to bring the faith to our people and not just see how they conform to our systems when they need something from us.

Wouldn't it be wonderful if everyone experienced church as a place...

- to become aware of our identity as God's beloved sons and daughters;

- to enter into the dream of what can be when we all live in love;

- to encounter Christ through Word, sacrament, and the presence of one another;

- to be comforted in times of pain, challenged in times of self-centeredness, and renewed for the journey at all times;

- to share our gifts;

- to join others in bringing God's love to the entire world?

Instead, for far too many people the experience of church has become dismal, boring, judgmental, and, to say the least, unhelpful. Rather than coming on a regular basis to be nourished and support others, people come only for the basics of what they need and cannot get elsewhere: the sacraments. Three of those sacramental moments happen during their young adult years: their marriage and the baptism and first communion of their children.

If you listen to young adults as they talk about these sacramental moments in their lives and in the lives of their siblings and friends, they will

Church attendance

In 1998, Fr. Terry Keehan, pastor of St. Matthias Church in Chicago, took an interesting sabbatical. For six months, he traveled coast to coast, interviewing Catholic young adults about their reasons for attending—and not attending—church on Sunday. Highlights of those interviews are included in Appendix A. Here are the top answers in each category, in the order of frequency with which that response was mentioned.

Why Catholic Young Adults Go to Church:

1. I want to experience community (38 percent).
2. It's a place to find meaning and strength (17.5 percent).
3. I want to pray/stay close to God (17 percent).
4. I go to receive holy communion (14 percent).
5. It feeds my spiritual hunger (10 percent).
6. It is a habit or an obligation (9 percent).
7. My church has good liturgy or good music (7.5 percent).

Why Catholic Young Adults Do Not Go to Church:

1. I'm too busy (28 percent).
2. I disagree with one or several of the church's teachings, for example, birth control, ban on women's ordination, celibate priesthood (23 percent).
3. I was forced to go as a child (14.5 percent).
4. I'm too lazy (13.5).
5. There's too much ritual (13.5 percent).

tell you that they appear to be the "enemy" at these times. What should be moments of gracious welcome and catechetical learning and celebrations of life and love are all too often occasions of legalistic nightmares, behavioral scrutiny, and liturgical dogmatism.

We are not operating private religious country clubs, where you take out your membership, pay your dues, and receive perks. The encounter with the local parish at significant sacramental, human moments is more than meets the eye. Through the ministry we show young adults in the local parish that they can experience the rich traditions of the entire Catholic Church. Many ministers are correct when they say, "I don't see them again after they get married." But if they are treated kindly and this significant human and sacramental moment is celebrated well, it is likely they will not forget this contact with the Catholic Church. Many of these encounters with young adults are their first experiences of the Catholic Church as adults. They are much more than just experiences with the local parish. Good parish ministry can begin a very positive adult relationship with the whole Catholic Church. We can exemplify and help others experience the spirit of Catholicism. A good experience for people at this time can last a lifetime, even for affiliative Catholics. A battle waged over rules, requirements, and laws stricter than Canon Law can go a long way to keep people in the back of the Sunday congregation, on the edge of the Catholic community, and out of the collection. Another young adult observed:

> *It never ceases to amaze me how every parish has a life of its own. Some parishes are so very full of life, while others seem to hang on by a thread. I am concerned that without a strong drive to motivate and educate pastors and others in parish leadership positions, little can be done to improve the relationship between young adults and the church. The mentality of "you have to do it this way . . ." or "Canon Law says . . ." has to go before positive change can come.*
>
> *The church is a community of human beings. The key word to me is "human." Therefore if the church is to be successful, its image should resemble that of a person—alive, feeling, thinking, acting. Too often young adults view the church as either nonexistent in their lives or as a powerful and sometimes unapproachable organization without feeling and without a face. If it desires a better relationship with its younger people, it must come alive and become human in their eyes.*

The Catholic Church has an image problem in the eyes of many young adults. But our church has always had an image problem; the crucifixion of the Lord Jesus testifies to that fact. Regardless of the perceived image, a healthy, positive experience of the local parish can change everything.

Photo by Peggy Scholl

Every summer, Cardinal Francis George celebrates Mass with young adults. Afterward he graciously invites them to a picnic on the lawn of his residence.

That image can be very personal, long remembered, and life-giving. Positive experiences of care, welcome, kindness, and compassion make all the difference and go a long way toward responding to the young adult who asked, "Does my presence here make any difference to anyone?"

Celebrating moments of healing and forgiveness, life and death, love and commitment, fear and hope can have a life-changing impact on young adults. So why does the testimony of so many Catholics tell us that such positive experiences are hard to find in our parishes? The following are typical observations of young adults:

> *We need to feel wanted and welcomed. We want to participate, but many times we need to be asked. We need to be given the opportunity to explore how we can fit into this thing called parish.*

> *To reach out to young adults, the parish must first and foremost foster a sense of community. That spirit must begin with parish leadership. Each parish should actively recruit its most talented young adults to help them lead this effort rather than simply relying on volunteers.*

Most parishes, whether city or suburb, are populated by families (young and old). The messages I have heard in these churches have been related to having a family. Beyond that, the sermons are stale; the priests do not do a good job relating the Gospel to daily life. All the announcements relate to married life and children. A goal would be that every parish would be a warm and welcoming place where young adults' needs would be met. The parish would have a welcoming atmosphere for all who attend.

People are hungry to experience the Catholic faith more than they are to debate it. Yet without good experiences, we are left with the headlines, the barroom gossip, and the horror stories passed on from one person to another.

What should be in place in our local church is clear: good, many, and varied expressions and experiences of the Catholic Church. Call it "parishness." This is what we heard from the parent of a young adult:

Personally, I think many young adults don't realize what they are missing from a strong parish community, because they came along when the parish communities were in decline; they missed the fun. The whole country is full of twenty-one-year-old kids who don't go to church on Sunday. Why? I think it's because they lacked "parishness" in their formative years. . . . We're dying to pass that sense of parish on to our children, and, hopefully, they will do the same.

What should be in place? That's simple: a greater sense of belonging, pride, and fun. Let's lighten it up just a bit and not take ourselves too seriously. Let's focus on that sense of belonging for which so many people hunger today. Let's make hospitality a virtue. Let's make our outreach to young adults a priority, our invitation gracious, and our welcome sincere. They are not strangers, but friends. They are not our enemies, but our very own people—all too often waiting to be welcomed so that they too can proudly and faithfully speak a strong vibrant "Amen" to the Body of Christ.

Maybe it's time that all segments of the Catholic Church interested in regenerating our parishes, activities, organizations, and programs adopt a simple yet essential strategy: a preferential option for our own young adult people. A preferential option would mean that when it comes time to seek new members, additional participants, and more volunteers, young adults, people in their twenties and thirties, married and single, would be the targeted group. We will opt for them first and foremost. We will make an invitation to them a priority over all others.

Before discussing strategies, we'll take a closer look at the young adults we are trying to reach. The more we know about who they are and how they respond, the better we'll be able to reach them.

Chapter 3

Getting to Know Young Adults

The term "young adult" can be problematic because it has several different definitions. Go to your local bookstore or public library and ask to be directed to the "young adult" section. You will find yourself standing in front of books written for preadolescents. At the other end of the spectrum, some people have difficulty admitting that they are no longer *young* adults and cling to the term well into their forties. To complicate matters further, in many parishes the term "young adult" is incorrectly defined as "singles." In order to avoid any misunderstandings about whom you are trying to serve, it is necessary to define the term "young adult" often whenever you use it.

In the Archdiocese of Chicago, we use this simple definition: *Young adults are women and men in their twenties and thirties, married and single.* Take notice of two parts: (1) twenties and thirties, and (2) married and single. Our approach in young adult ministry is to *an age in life,* not *a state in life* (exclusively married or single).

Young adults pose one of the greatest challenges to the church and society today and to anyone in a leadership position who tries to call them together. But here are some points to keep in mind as you consider what might be possible in your situation.

• Young adults are the group that has withdrawn more than any other age group to the edge of the institutional church and of many other segments of the culture. Yet the journey through the young adult years is one of reestablishing ties with many segments of the culture, the church included.

• The three main areas of interest among young adults are relationships, spirituality, and work. They long for intimacy—to be loved and have others to love—and they search for a community (church-related

17

or not) that shares their values and interests. They seek meaning in their lives and want to connect more deeply with the Source of Life. They are highly talented and skilled, and doing meaningful work is important to them. They generously share their time and talent as they seek to build a better world.

• Because people move through life at their own pace, there is no guarantee that young adults will be in a particular place at the statistically defined time. In other words, not everyone at the age of twenty-two will be indifferent to your work in establishing a young adult group, just as not everyone aged twenty-eight to thirty-one will be standing in line to attend their first young adult activity.

• An increasing number of young adults have had very positive church experiences in their college years, thanks to excellent campus ministry programs. Others have connected during earlier years in parishes—good family experiences of faith and church, good school years, positive memories of a parish youth group, or a memorable high school or college retreat experience. We can easily build on these positive experiences. These women and men will be excited to discover new church experiences during their young adult, postcollege years. They have already experienced the church as a place to meet good people and grow deeper in faith. A young adult group is their next developmental experience as Catholics.

• Many young adults have had minimal church contact during their earlier years. Fewer Catholic schools, less time in religious education programs, and minimal involvement with high school youth groups or religious education programs have left these young adults with little first-hand experience of the value of the church. Yet, many hunger for the meaning of the tradition.

• Some young adults who are returning to church practices are quickly disillusioned with the church. They are different now from the way they were as children. Going to church with your parents is certainly different from going by yourself. Once someone has stopped attending church for an extended period of time, it is hard to come back. Also, expectations are high. What they seek is not easily found: a place to worship (with preaching and music to which they can relate), a spiritual home, people with whom to build community, and opportunities to help build a better world.

• Until they have a good experience, it is difficult to attract young adults to prayer-driven events (retreats, special Masses, small faith groups).

Although young adults are deeply spiritual, they express little interest in "churchy" things. They simply might be seeking to gather with people their age who share their values, and they know that church groups can attract good people. For this group, church-sponsored social events might be a better place to start. We will talk more about this in chapter 5: "Organizing a Parish Young Adult Group."

• Even with the most personal invitation, some young adults will not participate in a church-sponsored young adult group because of deep-seated stereotypes about church, church groups, and the type of young adults who participate. "It's for losers and weirdos," or, "Those things are for holy-rollers and Bible beaters." It is going to take a direct, personal invitation and a very positive experience to get beyond such stereotypes.

• Young adult groups can attract an inordinate number of needy people: people who are incredibly shy, people with few if any friends, people who seem chronically depressed, and people who just have a hard time relating to their peers. Although the church has a responsibility to care for all people, you cannot begin with this group. Only after a strong, healthy core group of young adults is established will you be able to support those with greater needs. A strategy for calling together those strong, healthy people is also presented in chapter 5.

• Some young adults approach a young adult group or gathering confused about life. It is not unusual for the parents of some of these people to make all the arrangements for their presence. After all, the church is a good place to help them find friends and work out their problems. Without realizing it, some may come looking for therapy to help with their problems. Although gathering with other young adults can certainly have therapeutic value, that is not the purpose of young adult ministry. Those whose agenda is to obtain help with their personal problems will need to be directed to qualified professionals.

• Some young adults will approach a young adult gathering with a very rigid and close-minded set of expectations. They might carry a heavy spiritual agenda. They want—and will do all they can to get—Bible study. The group had better do it! Some might carry an intense social justice agenda. The group is of value only if it takes a strong anti-nuclear stand and eliminates all sexist language. In the name of truth, some may try to impose rigid doctrinal and liturgical practices on their peers and church ministers. Such types might not be open to where other people are in life.

The key here will be to clearly define the goal (and dream) of young adult ministry in your situation.

• Others show up out of curiosity. A lot of people will come *once* to check things out. What kinds of people have come (younger, older, healthy, needy, all single, primarily women, a good balance)? How many? What are they talking about? Will they care if I am there? The curious, who really are not sure why they came, must be made to feel welcome and appreciated. There is a great deal of positive energy when healthy young people gather. First impressions when people enter the room mean a great deal.

These observations about young adults, their world, and their relationship to the church are not presented to discourage people or burst any bubbles of enthusiasm and hope. They are presented to spell out the pragmatic philosophy of Professor Harold Hill in *The Music Man:* "You gotta know the territory!"

PART TWO

YOUNG ADULTS
AND THE PARISH

Chapter 4

Integrating Young Adults
into the Life of the Parish

Often when parish leaders decide it is time to do more for their young adults, they think in terms of starting a new program. Although that is certainly an option, there is an easier, more natural, and more immediate response: *integrate young adults into the existing life of the parish.* This is a worthy goal for any parish, and it makes sense. Young adults are searching for meaning in their lives. Parish life is the place Catholics delve into what matters most: faith, family, what it means to be fully alive, how to live as Christians, discernment of one's vocation, to name a few. At the heart of the Catholic tradition is Eucharist, where we receive the Body of Christ and grow in communion with one another. Could there be a better place to find meaning than where we connect with the Source of Life and one another?

When a parish functions effectively, members support one another as they grow in faith and develop their gifts. The role of the priests and all other leaders is to support the laity as they work to make a difference in the world beyond the parish doors. Since a parish is intergenerational, people of all ages learn from one another. Young adults benefit greatly by being active members of the parish community. Conversely, the parish community benefits greatly by receiving and nurturing the gifts and skills of young adults.

Listen to what some young adults have said about parish life:

My parish seems to serve two groups of people: families with school-aged children and senior citizens.

I walk in on Sunday knowing nobody, and I leave knowing nobody.

When are they going to learn that they can't have it both ways? They sit and complain that there are no younger people around. When we tried to get involved, they made it clear it had to be their way.

A lot of it is my problem. I stopped going to church quite a while ago. It's hard to come back. I don't want to feel awkward.

Someone should tell them to change their language. Almost every time I go to Mass someone says, "Welcome to our parish family." How can they be my family when I don't fit in?

They told me that before I could schedule a date for my wedding I had to be an active member of the parish for six months.

I was a communion minister when I was away at college. I called someone about doing that in this parish. So far, no one has gotten back to me.

Why don't I get involved? That's easy. There's nothing there for me.

Something has gone terribly wrong when young adults, who used to be the backbone of parish organizations, are not present, do not feel like they fit in, or cannot seem to break into the parish structure. What young adult ministry can do for those in their twenties and thirties is help them understand that they are an important part of our church. Whether they are single or married, with or without children, and whether the parish warmly greets them and makes them feel welcome or not, they are an important part of our church. Parishes and other faith communities need to learn to embrace and support young adults if they want them to become integrated into parish life.

One difficulty is that for so long our parishes have concentrated on school-aged children and senior citizens. Now that young adults are marrying and having children later than ever before, they do not stay connected through family programs that, in fact, are not for them. Unless we make a conscious effort to let members of this age group know their presence is important, we will lose them. We have already lost many to fundamentalist churches that are quick to embrace them. Personally greeting them on Sunday can go a long way. Direct personal invitation to participate in the liturgical ministries of the parish can also have a great impact. Begin Sunday Mass by asking those present to welcome one another to church and introduce themselves to someone they don't know. This can have

Young adults have a great deal of life, joy, talent, and energy to bring to our church. This weekend retreat was entitled: "Creating a Spirit to . . . Work Like You Don't Need the Money, Dance Like Nobody's Watching, Love Like You've Never Been Hurt, Sing Like No One Is Listening, and Live Like It's Heaven on Earth!"

an immediate positive impact, especially on young adults who might not know anyone else in church that day. Why should they participate in an organization that does not meet their needs, does not seem to appreciate the gifts they bring, does not extend gracious hospitality, provides unnecessary hoops through which to jump if they do approach to ask about marriage or baptism, and holds on to leadership positions so tightly that there really is no place for them to share their time and talent?

Another difficulty is that some people in leadership positions in our church and parishes prefer to keep things as they have always been. That is fine if what has always been continues to work well. But sometimes a new strategy is necessary. Our world is changing quickly; "business as usual" is no longer producing desired results. The Second Vatican Council was a good example of the church examining its position on a number of issues and forging new paths where they made sense. Now, in each of our parishes, organizations, and communities, it is time to decide what new paths are necessary in dealing with young adults.

Below is a seven-stage plan for any parish interested in regenerating its congregation, liturgy, and organizational life. If all the various commissions and organizations of the parish are committed to regenerating the parish, major strides can be made.

Stage 1: Reputation

What are people saying about your parish or organization? To find out about the parish's reputation, don't ask the staff members, and don't ask the parishioners who sit in the first three rows on Sunday. Ask your regular "pew people"; they are your loyal ones, and they also listen. If you're very brave, you can try to tap the people on the margins; seek out and talk to young adults who don't frequent the parish often. How easy is it to get involved? What do people say about the congregation? How easy is it to get married? How easy is it to get your child baptized? What's the gossip about cliques? Is parish governance really interested in caring for the needs of all? You need to begin with what people are thinking and saying about the place. Whether it's true or not does not matter. You need to know how people perceive the parish. Be aware that this can be very threatening to the leadership. You have to work through that. If you do not know what is being said about you, you don't know what issues to address and what components may need to be changed. Often those of us on the inside lose touch with the people on the fringe, and that's who we need to find a way to serve.

Here is one e-mail that came into the diocesan Young Adult Ministry Office about an experience a young adult had at her parish:

About a month ago, in my perkiest voice possible, I called the associate pastor (I chose him because he works with the RCIA group, which had a lot of young people). I asked him whether he knew of any young adults in the parish, through RCIA or elsewhere, that would be interested in joining forces with me to create some kind of young adult group. I emphasized that I was interested in taking on the work, not asking him to do anything but refer me to kindred souls. After a month of repeated follow-up voice mail messages (none returned), I finally received a letter in the mail (apparently he couldn't be courteous enough to communicate the news "in person" by telephone). The letter said that the Parish Life Commission would need to "supervise" such a group, and they were unwilling to, so they had essentially rejected the idea of a ministry to young adults (of course with the usual flowery words of "not at this time . . . "). Can anyone on your staff recommend a "young adult friendly" Catholic church in my area? Thanks. Elizabeth

Is your parish "young adult friendly" or do you have the reputation of catering to young families or another sector of the population? Is the congregation viewed as young or old? Is the leadership open to trying new things when opportunities present themselves? (Many parishes have not had the good fortune to have someone like Elizabeth come forward.) Once you know how you are perceived, you have a starting point for changing inaccurate perceptions and moving forward based on your strengths.

Stage 2: Inventory

Taking inventory means determining who is involved in all parish activities and organizations. This is not just a body count ("We have twenty catechists, thirty-two Eucharistic ministers, fifteen ushers, and twelve ministers of care"). You need to know how many people are involved by both age and state in life. For example, how many teens, twenties, thirties, forties people are involved? How many senior citizens are active? How many of the leaders and participants of parish activities and organizations are single, married, single again? How many are parents, and how many are single parents? *Look for the presence and involvement of young adults at every level of parish life.* Such an inventory will soon reveal who is present and who is absent—both in terms of age and state in life. Some inventories will show that the parish is being governed by people all beyond middle age. Other results might reveal that the presence of women and men in their twenties is necessary to give balance to the religious education program. A mix of various ages and lifestyles can make the parish more inviting and responsive to the needs of its own members.

A parish asked us to assist their staff and parish council in encouraging their young adults to become more present and active. One person at that meeting later said, "You know, since you gave us your suggestion, I have been taking inventory. I didn't realize that there are hardly any younger people involved in distributing holy communion and reading at our church. The Sunday afternoon Mass is all younger people in the congregation, and all older people around the altar." She understood. Watch the ages and life experiences of your catechists as well. Who are they? Can you seek to get a balance of men and women, parents and nonparents, single and married, college students and workers, young adults and older adults? Pay attention to who is present and active, and who is not. Look to see if single parents have a place. Many believe they are not welcome at this time in their lives. Be very concerned about noncustodial fathers. You see them one Sunday with their children; the next, they are without them. Can we integrate them into the Sunday worship? To do so would be a sign to the congregation of who should be involved in the life of the parish: *everybody*.

See where young adults are and are not connected. How many young adults are liturgical ministers? How many are on the parish council? How about the finance committee? These people have important positions in the workforce, but when it comes to church, we often overlook their gifts.

Stage 3: Integration

Integration is the strategy of adding young adults to the parish organizations and events that lack their presence. Our congregations will be healthier if we can integrate people of all ages and lifestyles. The question to be asked at this stage is: Where could young adults be participating, but they aren't? The challenge then is to make a conscious effort to get young adults involved in those positions.

If on Sunday mornings at your parish, there are no young adult lectors, ushers, greeters, Eucharistic ministers, gift bearers, musicians, or cantors, set a new goal. If one-third of the parish members are young adults, strive to have one-third of the liturgical ministers be young adults by this time next year. Do the same for your catechists. The way to meet that goal is described in the next stage, invitation.

Stage 4: Invitation

The best method for integrating young adults into parish life is direct personal invitation. We call this the *Jesus Method of Organizing.* Jesus hand-

Who are your ministers?

Every first Sunday of the month, we invite young adults throughout the archdiocese to a Mass and continental breakfast in the parish hall. One Sunday, after consecrating the bread and wine, the celebrant turned to give communion to the Eucharistic ministers and realized that not one was under the age of forty. We vowed never to let that happen again. Now we have two young adult volunteers who are responsible for inviting all the ministers for that Mass and making sure they are all young adults. Each person is personally asked to help and then is mailed a thank-you note. We nurture young adults and their relationship to church. Sometimes we have to lobby for younger people. We have to call together the leadership, point out the way things are, and give leaders suggestions for making changes. Where places are serious about caring for their young people, things change.

picked his apostles. They responded to the invitation, "Follow me." Many young adults are eager to be involved in their parishes. However, they need to be invited. Since they see few people their age involved, they conclude that they are not needed or welcome to participate in those leadership roles. Putting an announcement in the parish bulletin falls short; it leaves you at the whim of whoever comes to help. In all likelihood, you will get volunteers, but probably not young adults. If you are looking for women and men in their twenties and thirties, begin by creating an invitation list of the young adults the parish leaders know. Who would they like to see in various positions of leadership? By personally inviting those you want to participate in various activities, you are increasing the possibility that they will become more involved. You will then have a higher degree of assurance of getting the desired intergenerational mix of people for parish life and activities.

Stage 5: Separate but Similar

For various reasons, some parish programs and activities cannot be regenerated with new and younger people. Young adults are not a comfortable fit in parish organizations where everyone is as old as their grandparents

Timing is everything!

If your parish is sincerely interested in being more diverse in lifestyle and age, the parish staff and key committee members might need to alter how the system schedules, assigns, and uses the time and talent of younger people. Young adults cannot usually give you the same type of commitment that older adults can. Their personal, school, and work schedules are busy and constantly changing. A more effective way to reach people and obtain their support for a specific task is to ask for commitment of a defined short period of time.

For example, young adults will typically not know if they are available to serve as lector at the 10 a.m. Mass six weeks from now. They will also not be able to commit to helping for the next consecutive six weeks. We suggest that those who seriously want to integrate younger people into liturgical positions keep a specific number of slots open for them. Have someone responsible for filling those slots one week in advance. The usual system of sending out postcards and asking people to state their availability a month or two in advance just does not work with young adults. Have your list ready, and personally invite them when you need them.

and working on the timetable of retirees. Rather than letting go of the good work being done by such groups as the Holy Name Society and the Altar and Rosary Society, young adults might consider an organization with a new name, a nuanced purpose, and a much younger average age of participants. For example, not everyone needs to be a part of the St. Vincent de Paul Society in order to serve the needs of the poor in the parish and the larger community. A separate organization with a new title can be very attractive in gathering young adults for engaging in volunteer work and building community.

This concept of separate but similar also can be applied to specific support groups. It can make more sense to create a group for younger Catholics who share an experience than it does to incorporate them into an already existing group. For example, even though the parish has a strong widow/widowers group, it makes sense to create a widow/widowers group for women and men in their twenties and thirties. Young adults who have lost a spouse have

Sometimes it's oil and water

Two young men came in to talk about the Holy Name Society. They were frustrated. Their fathers had participated in the Holy Name Society, and these young men found the work of the organization worthwhile. They also liked the idea of spending time with other men. After hearing from their fathers and other men in the Holy Name Society that younger guys just do not care, they convinced a few of their friends to give it a try. They attended several meetings and tried to get involved. But the by-laws were written thirty years ago, and the current leaders had enough votes to keep everything their way, and they did.

Not everything can or should be integrated. Sometimes it is necessary to start something different. Create a men's society for younger men. Let them start over and make new by-laws. Give the group a name, and let them do more good work. We need to keep finding ways to build a better world. If younger people can no longer achieve their goals in such classic, well-established groups, they need to begin new groups. Let's not be paralyzed by any structure we've created.

very little in common with our seniors who lost their spouses some years ago but enjoy each other's company. A group for married couples is a good idea, but those in their twenties and thirties, who are still trying to discover how marriage works, will have questions and concerns very different from those who have been married over a decade. To create a space in which young adults can explore those questions and concerns among themselves is a wonderful goal. Again, begin with what you hear from people. If three couples express an interest in gathering with other young couples, you are off to a good start. Small Christian communities for young adults also make sense. Such groups allow them to meet their peers in the parish, support one another, and share their faith as they deal with common issues.

Stage 6: Occasional Activities

Recently a woman in her twenties said, "My time has become more precious than gold." Between long work hours, school, relationships, and various other commitments, young adults are especially busy people. They will make time for things that are important to them, but they may be reluctant to participate in parish activities that require a large time commitment. Participation on four consecutive nights at a parish mission or a six-week-long parish formation program will be out of the question for many of them. They simply do not have the time. Even if the activity directly responds to a need, if the time commitment is great, their participation is difficult, if not impossible. This is not to say that older adults aren't equally busy or more so, but that young adults are reluctant to take on tasks they don't think they can give their all to.

One of the most effective principles in young adult ministry is "less is more" (see chapter 5). A few opportunities handled well have a greater chance of success with young adults than many activities or doing anything over a long period of time.

In the Catholic Church we often "create a new group" in response to a particular need. This is a good option if you have a heavy concentration of young adults and they have the leadership skills to make the group work well. If you do not have the need or resources to create a new group, consider offering occasional activities.

Any way you choose to gather young adults will send a clear message that they are an important part of the church and that their presence is valued. The more often you gather them, the better you will become at hearing what they want and responding to their needs. After you integrate young adults into leadership positions, they will help find ways and places to plug in other young adults. Don't be concerned about quantity; go for quality.

Stage 7: New Movements

In their own day, the Legion of Mary and the Holy Name Society prepared for the first-ever meetings of their new and exciting organizations. There is a good chance that the leaders of those new Catholic organizations were young adults. These leaders were excited about working through the church to respond to a need in our society.

What about today? What are the needs in our world to which a new Catholic activity might respond? Within the church or parish, what do young adults, married or single, want to see happen? How about a group

Additional ideas

There is no need to have a young adult event in your parish every week or even every month. Consider the following:

1. Conduct a speaker series that lasts no more than four weeks. Make sure it deals with issues important to young adults and at a time that is good for them. Do one summer program and one winter program.

2. For those who want more, begin some young adult small faith groups.

3. Host a going-away party for those leaving home for college. Such an event could connect those headed for the same schools who might not know one another and assure everyone of the parish's blessing and support.

4. Be seasonal. Host an Advent or Lenten Day of Reflection for young adults.

of Catholic men joining forces to serve as male role models for fatherless children? There are many possibilities.

Even in the glory days of the Catholic Church in the United States (some would say the 1950s), the parish couldn't do it all. As good as parishes were, many Catholics found their "church" experience through movements like the Christian Family Movement, Serra Clubs, the Cana Conference, the Cursillo Movement, the Catholic Interracial Council, the Catholic Council on Working Life, the St. Vincent de Paul Society, Young Christian Workers, Young Christian Students, and the Catholic Youth Organization. These movements, both as part of and independent from parish life, added much to the faith life and the Catholic identity of our people. With so many of these movements gone now, the burden of offering people a good Catholic experience rests almost solely with the local parish. Today's parish has unrealistic expectations placed upon it. It cannot be all things to all people. It never was in the past. Can we create new forms of Catholic expression and identity? Would a diocesan outreach to young adults make sense? Is it time in our church to create a young adult "movement"? Should several neighboring parishes join resources to create an areawide young adult ministry program?

A group of young adults enjoy each other's company in conversation during the annual FOCUS conference.

Creating a new movement begins by asking, "What is needed?" Remember that all the tradition-bound organizations, like the Knights of Columbus and the Daughters of Isabella, at one time were put together to respond to new moments in life. Mainly staffed by younger people, they met human and spiritual needs. What today in your diocese or congregation is needed but isn't there? Where could or should there be a new movement? The next step is to gather some people and take the risk—call it a pilot program.

One of the greatest joys of working in ministry is exploring new possibilities. Once a parish makes a commitment to young adults, invites them into leadership positions, and offers them quality experiences, it is time to look at what else might be possible. This generation of young adults is the most highly educated group of people this world has ever seen. They are also incredibly skilled and generous when asked. Gather some of the young adult leaders and brainstorm about *what could be* in place in your parish for this age group. Then use their talents to help get there. Never forget that young adults are *adults,* and that their parents, when in their twenties and thirties, were the backbone of most parish organizations. Our goal could be to have a committee of young adults reaching out to their

Church life and young adults

The activities, topics, and offices listed below are opportunities for connecting with young adults and inviting them into greater participation.

Parish activities focusing primarily on young adults:

RCIA
Marriage preparation
Weddings
Baptism preparation
Baptism

Activities into which young adults can easily be integrated:

Parish governance
Catechesis
Liturgical ministries
Marriage enrichment
Adult religious education
Family programs (CFM)
Divorce support groups (Phoenix)
Small Christian communities
Athletic programs
Men's and women's organizations
AA, ACOA, Twelve-step programs
Preschool parent programs

Issues targeted to young adults:

Relationship, intimacy
Social programs
Work and career issues
Catholic formation
Evangelization
Spirituality
Volunteerism

Archdiocesan resources for young adult ministry:

Young Adult Ministry Office
Evangelization Office
Office for Catechesis
Ministry in Higher Education
Office of Divine Worship
Family Ministry Office
Phoenix Ministry
Social Service Agencies

peers and inviting them into greater participation in their church. It would not take long for the reputation of this "young adult friendly" parish to spread.

Chapter 5

Organizing a Parish Young Adult Group

A second approach to young adult ministry is to create an effective parish-based young adult group. Though the integration of young adults into the overall life of the parish should be a high priority, many young adults express a need to connect with their peers under the auspices of their church.

When we ask young adults what they are looking for in their church, the most frequent answers we hear are:

I want to meet people my age who share my values.

I want to share my concerns about faith with others in my age group; I don't want to live my faith alone.

I am looking for people who have similar beliefs and values, people to have lasting friendships with.

My goal is meeting and establishing relationships with other young adults.

There are not enough programs directed at young adults. We need to feel more included. Don't just tell me there is "a lack of interest" in the parish.

I'm looking for a welcoming church for young adults. Where are the groups in which I can meet others the same age, with the same background?

I want to meet other young adults to share my faith with. This helps me to continue and grow in my journey of faith.

Where Do We Begin? People before Programs

Very often when the idea of beginning a young adult group in a parish is conceived, a few well-intentioned leaders get together, and several first steps are taken. A bulletin announcement inviting young adults to attend a group planning meeting or a printed announcement to attend an initial event is prepared. It usually reads something like this:

> All young adults interested in starting a young adult group in our parish are invited to a meeting this Tuesday evening at 8:00 in the parish center. Bring a friend!

With great apprehension, the leaders wait to see who comes. All too often those leaders leave the parish center greatly disappointed. "How did it go?" "It didn't go all that well." "It's not what we thought it would be." "There should have been more people." "Where were all the good people?" "People didn't really seem to have a good time." "Now what do we do?" Back to the drawing board . . . maybe. That is, back to the drawing board if those organizers are not too discouraged to try again.

Young adult groups should *not* begin with a meeting, an event, or even a bulletin announcement. They should begin with the dream of who will make up the young adult group. That dream can be found excitedly residing in the minds of the organizers. In other words, a young adult group begins when the leaders can answer specifically and concretely this question: Who do you want to be there?

The answer is not simply young adults in the parish. What type of young adults? Single? Married? Young professionals? Social activists? College grads? All Catholic? All "church types"? All men? All women? All friends of one another? What ages? All twenty-year-olds? All over thirty? How many? Four people? Forty people? Four hundred people?

In other words, before announcing any activity, event, or meeting, the organizers must be able to articulate a profile of the group they wish to form. If that is accomplished, the profile will answer the first question: *Who do we want to be the foundation of this young adult group?*

Next, the organizers should begin an invitational outreach to young adults who fit that profile. A successful young adult group should not be left to chance or put in the hands of whoever shows up. Before the first meeting or activity, there is a lot of work to be done. When the people who fit the profile are invited and gather together, any young adult activity— from the very beginning—has a better chance of being successful. That is basic common sense. It is also the articulation of our first principle of ministerial organization: *With the right people, you can watch the grass grow and have a good time.*

Strategies of Invitation:
How to Find and Recruit the Right People

Once a concrete and very specific profile is established, the strategy for recruiting those people is based on another principle: *The best strategy of invitation is to proceed from the known to the unknown, to move from the most personal to the impersonal.* At first glance that seems obvious, but many leaders choose to begin with an impersonal bulletin announcement inviting unknown people to a meeting. Here is a better way to proceed:

Step 1: Keeping in mind the profile of who you want to participate, determine which young people who fit the profile are **known personally** by the organizers. Parish staff, lay leaders, and key parish volunteers should also be asked: "We are forming a young adult group in our parish. We want to start and build our group with twenty young adults who are in their mid- to late twenties, single or married. Who in that group do you know personally?"

As you answer that question, a list of young adults will emerge. This list might include young adults living outside the parish. It might include personal friends, co-workers, and neighbors. It might include sons and daughters (married and single) of parish leaders who live outside the parish now, but still call the parish home. Add to that list the young adults who were married recently, just had a child baptized, or completed the RCIA program within the past several years. The list might include other nonresident people such as undergraduate or graduate college students, and women and men in military or volunteer service (Peace Corps, Jesuit Volunteer Corps). At this stage, you are not developing that list based on anyone's availability to attend anything. You are simply collecting names of young adults who fit the profile and are personally known by parish leaders.

Personally known people are most easily contacted and potentially the strongest people around whom to develop a young adult group. If you can clearly articulate to others the type of young adults you are looking for, and they, in response, can give you the names of young adults they know who fit the profile, the odds of a good beginning increase.

Step 2: Develop a list of young adults from the **parish census forms.** Parish records are usually organized by year of birth. Again, keep in mind the profile of who you are seeking to invite to the young adult group.

You may hear the comment, "Why bother? Young adults don't register!" As true as that may be, taking names from parish census forms can be very revealing. First, it might help determine an approximate number of young adults who are in the parish. Recently a parish of 2,000 families made a list of all their people between the ages of twenty and forty. The final list had 1,875 names on it. Given that many young adults in fact do not register, imagine how many are actually living in the parish!

The task at hand is to collect names of young adults who potentially can be contacted for young adult activities. Census forms will reveal the names of young adults who have registered in the parish on their own. They will give you the names of young adults who appear on their parents' registration forms, whether they still live at home or not. They will list single people and married young adults, with and without children.

A census list of young adults will reveal something else too. Take the list to the parish staff and parish leaders. Ask them to initial the names of people they know. This list will then generate more personally known young adults who can be contacted and invited to what is being planned.

Step 3: Collect past **parish school and religious education program rosters.** Who is known and remembered on those lists?

Step 4: Who do other people know? In casual conversation with people where you live, work, and worship, tell them who you are looking to attract. Then ask them who they know. Remember that you are simply collecting names of young adults who fit your profile. This list might include friends of friends, apartment dwellers not registered, and young adult children who have returned home but are not currently registered in the parish.

Step 5: Collect names through **parish bulletin announcements.** In this situation, the Sunday bulletin is not being used to invite young adults to an event or to a young adult group meeting. Rather, it is being used simply to collect names. For example,

Our parish is making plans to develop activities for young adults, people in their twenties and thirties, married and single. If you are a young adult, if you have children who are young adults, or if you know of any young adults who might be interested in these activities, please send their names, addresses, and telephone numbers to the rectory in care of John Jones.

It's a good idea to run this type of announcement more than once. We suggest that four bulletin announcements be prepared and published for four consecutive weeks. One-time announcements are often missed.

Step 6: Solicit names and addresses of young adults from **places where they frequent:** grocery stores, laundromats, health clubs, restaurants, and bars. An example of a notice that might be posted:

St. Joan's Catholic Church has plans to develop activities for young adults, people in their twenties and thirties, married and single. If you are interested, or know someone who might be, please send name, address, and phone number to John Jones in care of St. Joan's Church, 123 Trinity Street, Chicago, IL 60600.

Step 7: Place an ad or have a story written in the **local community newspaper.** Have those who are interested send names and addresses to the contact person in care of the church.

The purpose of steps one through seven above is simply to gather the names and addresses of young adults who fit your profile. The next step will be to invite them to an initial meeting or activity. The strategy is to *proceed from the known to the unknown, moving from the personal to the impersonal.* These steps are not novel or extraordinarily creative; they are used all the time. Can you imagine a pastor who is interested in forming a parish finance committee putting this announcement in the bulletin:

Anyone in the parish interested in serving on a parish finance committee, please come to a meeting Tuesday night at 7:00 in the rectory. Bring a friend!

No way! The initial effort to establish a parish finance committee is by personal invitation to a few personally known trustworthy people. Why should the formation of a young adult group be anything less?

Young adult gatherings have a greater chance of success if the organizers have some knowledge of who will be present. It is not necessary to know everyone who will attend, but if most are known and fit the profile, the rate of success will be greater. For example, if the leaders expect a group of twenty young adults to attend and they personally can count on fourteen people they know, there will be less anxiety and a greater likelihood of success. The leaders know the needs and expectations of the majority. Conversely, if a group of twenty people arrives for an initial young adult gathering, and fourteen are unknown by the leaders, the possibility of success is greatly diminished. There are few shared concerns and previously agreed upon expectations. This initial gathering of young adults can be a friendly one, but it has a greater chance of ending with confusion and uncertainty. The dream of a young adult group will still rest (now less comfortably) in the minds and hearts of the leaders. They will still be seeking a group of young adults who will give some flesh, blood, spirit, and life to their idea of what a young adult group could be.

When the leaders can personally call together a majority of the group they wish to form, the plan and hope for the future is strong. It has a broad base of the type of people who the leaders know will give meaning and direction to what they want to accomplish. When young adults who fit the leaders' profile are present, the planners can breathe easier and channel their energy into building what can be. Moreover, the importance of the activities planned takes a comfortable back seat to the people present. When good people are present, good things happen. With the right group of people, you can watch the grass grow and have a good time.

The Jesus Method of Organizing

At first glance this process of hand-picking and personally inviting young adults to begin a young adult group seems elitist. It is elitist. Elitism is not necessarily wrong, especially in beginning programs.

Consider the beginning of the Christian movement. Jesus didn't put a sign on a palm tree saying:

All those who want to be apostles sign up here.

When Scripture recounts that Jesus read from the Book of Isaiah and all eyes were on him, Jesus doesn't say: "While I have your attention, there will be a meeting for those who want to form a group of apostles in this synagogue on Tuesday night at 7:30. Bring a friend."

There is a prevalent theory in church circles that groups affiliated with the church must be all things to all people. Indeed, there must be room for everybody who wants to attend—but not necessarily at the beginning. The "Jesus Method of Organizing" must be kept in mind. After walking through towns, he said, "You, you, and you, come on. Walk with me. I will make you fishers of people." The call of the apostles was by direct personal invitation. Later, after the development of the group and the movement, there was room for everybody. If you believe in something and hold it to be important, you do not leave it to fate or to whoever shows up to help. Dreams are fleshed out with great forethought and much planning.

If your goal for the formation of a young adult group is an important dream, do not leave it to chance. Do what the Lord did. Invite people. It works! We are the result of his personal, elitist invitation to follow him. It's our turn now. Let us go and do the same!

Here we can list our first three Principles of Organization:

#1   With the right people, you can watch the grass grow and have a good time.

#2   The best strategy of invitation is to proceed from the known to the unknown, to move from the most personal to the impersonal.

#3   The Jesus Method of Organizing is most effective. Gather people by direct, personal invitation.

A Young Adult Group Is Only as Good as Its Leadership

Leadership is the most critical issue in any organization. The second most critical issue is the type of people present. The third is what the group does. Often in church circles we work in the opposite order. We plan activities for people not yet gathered, with leadership that might not be able to respond adequately to the people who attend or to the activities they want to undertake. Below are some principles of leadership to keep in mind as you move forward:

1. Leadership is an aspect of a person's personality, not just an acquired skill.

The skills can be learned, but everyone in a leadership position has certain traits, styles, and strengths. As a leader, what do you like to do? What do you enjoy (social events, public speaking, hospitality, service opportunities, grunt work, detail work, spiritual enrichment, music, sports, drama)? As a leader, what don't you like to do? The activities of a young adult group and the people who will be invited and attracted will be based on the leader's personality, interests, and style of leadership.

Take a few minutes to answer these questions:

- What are three strengths you have as a leader?
- What would you rather avoid doing or planning for others?
- What type of people will be attracted by your personality?
- What type of people will you shy away from or avoid inviting?
- In spite of yourself, who do you want to attend?
- Who don't you want to be a part of the group?
- What activities (social, serious, spiritual, service) do you enjoy?
- What do you dislike?
- What could you tolerate if you had to?

We all have strengths and weaknesses. One of the first requirements of effective leadership is to know what those strengths and weaknesses are. It can also be helpful to have someone who knows us well answer the above questions for us. What we perceive to be our strengths, weaknesses, likes, and dislikes might be different from how others see us.

This is also a good exercise for the core group of leaders who are in the process of developing a young adult group. By knowing one another's likes, dislikes, strengths, and weaknesses, the core group will know who can respond to people's different interests and who has the desire to plan which type of activity. For example, if a group leader's dream is to create a small faith group, that person is probably not the best choice to organize the winter volleyball program.

2. Good leadership plans activities that balance quantity and quality.

Doing things well is more important than doing a lot of things. With any new endeavor like a young adult program, there is a tendency to undertake a lot of activities. Quantity alone will not guarantee success. As a matter of fact, it can work against a successful young adult group. For example, if you plan an activity for every Friday night for the next six months, you will attract people who have no social life outside the group. Those with active social lives might be discouraged from attending, and they might be the well-balanced people who can make a young adult group successful.

Less is more. A few well-planned activities are more effective than weekly events of great variety. Like so many others in our society, young adults are busy people. Their lives are occupied with many important commitments. They work hard and put in long hours. They have families, friends, and personal lives and a limited amount of free time. A parish young adult group should supplement and enhance young adults' lives.

3. Good leadership always tries to be gracious and hospitable.

On the surface that seems self-evident and a style all leaders would see as critically important. Yet sometimes another aspect of leadership surfaces: "Wow, did I work hard to get this ready for you!" or "Am I tired! I worked all day. I had so much to do for this young adult group that I had no time for dinner." The personal agenda of the leaders is not important to the participants. Ninety-nine percent of people work on the basis of their self-interest. Their self-interest is to have a worthwhile time at what they have chosen to attend. How hard leaders have worked is quite unimportant. Nor are participants doing the leaders a favor by attending a young adult activity.

The people present at an activity are much more than the result of the hard work that went into planning it. They are the incarnation— the lived-out dream—of what the young adult leaders have wanted from the beginning. Therefore, graciousness and gratitude are two of the most important behavior styles of the organizers. The leaders should be sure that *everyone* is welcomed and thanked during the course of every activity. There should be no complaining, no self-flattery, and no guilt—just graciousness and thanks.

4. Who leads and who should lead are two different issues.

Good leadership, in committees as well as in the group, cannot be left solely to the mercy of those who volunteer. *People must be called to leadership positions.* Not everyone has the skills necessary to get the job done. Others have the skills, but the style of their personality will offend more people than it will help. After a while, group leaders will know the "regulars" and can determine who to ask to do what. Since more people will need to be asked to do things than will ever volunteer, keep in mind that by asking for help you are inviting people to share their gifts and minister to their peers. Many young adults with very strong skills have never been given opportunities to share them in their church.

5. There are three basic styles of leadership: organizational, prophetic, and popular.

Two great Catholic organizers, Mr. Harry Fagan and Sr. Marjorie Tuite, O.P., have taught us that these three styles of leadership should be present in any effective group or organization.

Organizational leaders do the "grunt" work. They deal with such responsibilities as membership, publicity, budgets, letters, clean-up, schedules, and newsletters.

Prophetic leaders ask the tough questions. Why are we doing it this way? Where are all the people we wanted to attract? Why is this starting to go flat? Does it have to be done that way? In other words, nothing is presumed, and nothing is taken for granted.

Popular leaders reflect what people are saying, make people feel welcome, love to be with people, and exhibit much of the charm and graciousness needed for people to have a good time. An appropriate role for popular leaders during events is to begin at the front door welcoming people, then move into the room to work the crowd, and finally end up back at the door thanking people for coming.

No one person is good at all three—no one, not even you! Discuss the gifts and leadership styles of each leader, and the ways in which everyone can best share them.

6. Effective leaders must develop the skills of correction and intervention.

In every organization it will become necessary at times to tell certain people when they are out of line, their behavior is inappropriate, or they are at fault. This is the most difficult task for any leader. This action must always be taken with love, sincerity, and firmness. One strategy is to affirm the person while correcting the behavior. As kind as leaders try to be, however, it is not always possible to correct inappropriate behavior without pain and messiness. People will be hurt. Yet, if action is not taken when necessary, the behavior can lead to the quick demise of a young adult group. Inappropriate conduct, objectionable language, and negative attitudes have helped to destroy young adult groups, along with the dreams and hopes of the young adult leaders. What is painful in the short run can lead to life-giving results in the long run.

7. It is important to discover and nurture new leadership right from the beginning.

No one should be in charge forever. New leadership is healthy for any group. Right from the outset of a young adult group, the leaders should be seeking their replacements. One of the key ingredients of the young adult lifestyle today is mobility and change. Therefore, for a young adult group to survive for any length of time, it is imperative that the next generation of young adult leaders be sought out from the very beginning. When we move on, who will lead the group? If the future existence of a young adult group depends on the present leadership, it is not the best group it can be. If the goal is to help create a place where young adults can find support and attend activities with their peers in a church atmosphere, that goal should exist after the present leadership is long gone. If the leadership burns out and the group fades away, what has been accomplished? Keep in mind that this is the parish's young adult group, not the leaders' young adult group.

8. Leaders must train themselves to let go of people—even the best people.

When leaders have worked hard to develop a young adult group, participating in good programs and enjoying good times together, it is hard for the leaders to see key people move on with their lives. There is a tendency (often an unconscious one) on the part of leaders to "guilt" people into staying around or being present at events they do not particularly want to attend. There is also a tendency toward becoming overly possessive and working with only a few people that they like. Good leadership creates the freedom for people to give what they can when they can, and then to move on to other opportunities.

9. Leaders should analyze how they spend their time.

What percent of the leaders' time is spent doing what activities? Often what people think they spend time doing is different from what they actually do. To keep things moving smoothly, it might be helpful for leaders to ask themselves some of these questions:

- What percentage of time is used to reach out to new people?
- What percentage of time is used to plan?
- What percentage of time is used to execute plans?
- What percentage of time is spent with what percentage of people?

10. *Good leadership is sensitive to the spirit that is being communicated nonverbally.*

Watching a person's behavior tells more than listening to that person's words. For example,

- Do leaders communicate fun, excitement, and fascination in forming and working with a young adult group?
- Do leaders communicate a somber, overserious, overworked attitude?
- Are people in the group a burden or a joy to the leaders?
- Do the leaders communicate, nonverbally, joy and enthusiasm?

Remembering that any group is only as good as its leaders, do your best to be gracious and hospitable, to personally invite others into leadership positions, and to work off your own interests and gifts. The Christian spirit you convey will be contagious.

To our list of Principles of Organization, we can now add three more:

#1 With the right people, you can watch the grass grow and have a good time.

#2 The best strategy of invitation is to proceed from the known to the unknown, to move from the most personal to the impersonal.

#3 The Jesus Method of Organizing is most effective. Gather people by direct, personal invitation.

#4 A young adult group is only as good as its leaders.

#5 Less is more: doing a few things well far outweighs doing many things.

#6 Good leadership is gracious and hospitable and nurtures future leaders.

Hospitality

A common myth about church groups is that they are voluntary, that no one has to be there. The reality is that many church groups and meetings are not as voluntary as they appear. More than ever before, once you've signed up, your attendance is both expected and required. Consider some of these *not so voluntary* church groups and meetings: premarriage programs; baptismal preparation; first communion instruction; confirmation classes; service projects for candidates, parents, and sponsors; choir rehearsals; lector training; ministers of care meetings; religious education classes; RCIA.

The reality of a young adult group, however, is that no one has to be there. Young adults will come and participate because their self-interest is being served; their needs are being met. If that does not occur, all the time and effort invested is for naught. They will not return. Nothing can make them return. Their presence is *truly* voluntary. Since that is the case, hospitality is crucial.

At any gathering of young adults, the most essential element, after the actual presence of the people themselves, is *good hospitality*. Hospitality is that wonderful experience of being welcomed and feeling that your time and presence are truly appreciated.

The art of hospitality takes some skill and practice, but is not difficult. It begins with your own self-interest: how do you want to be greeted and treated when you walk into a gathering of strangers? In your answer to that question, you will find the basics of the art of hospitality.

If good hospitality takes place, you need not worry about covering all the important points you had planned. If people genuinely enjoy themselves and feel that their presence is appreciated, they will return. If the art of hospitality is lacking and people feel neglected or that their presence was taken for granted, all of the "important points" of your agenda and even the best planning will be in vain. People probably will not return.

We cannot assume that someone feels welcome. We might not realize, after a while, who the new people are. We forget that by spending time only with people we know, we might be judged a clique. We cannot assume that someone else has done the necessary greeting. As a leader, do it yourself. To determine whether hospitality has been achieved successfully, listen to the new voices and watch their facial expressions before they leave.

Their body language more than their words will tell you how successful you were.

You have multiple opportunities for extending good hospitality: at the beginning of an event, during the event, at the end of the event, and the day after the event.

Hospitality at the *beginning* of a young adult event means that you individually greet each person, ask each person's name, give your name, and inquire about each (if time permits, without snooping, with such questions as: Where do you live? on your own? at home? Where do you attend school? work? How long have you lived in the area? Any particular interests?). Introduce the newcomers to other people, and thank them for coming.

Hospitality *during* an activity means that you call people by name, move among the group, spend time with everyone, watch for loners, and listen for ideas, comments, and reactions.

Hospitality at the *end* of an activity means that you thank people for their time and presence, make sure everyone has a ride home, say good-bye by name, refrain from cleaning or clearing until everyone has left, spend time with those who wish to stay and talk, and extend a special word of thanks to key people (they may be your future leaders).

Hospitality the *day after* an activity means you mail a personal letter of thanks to all who were present and make a special phone call to your key people, whose continued presence is essential. The first reminder of the next gathering can be a part of your thank-you note.

Much of this material on hospitality might seem overly simple, self-evident, and routine. However, the little things are remembered, and hospitality is much more than a "little thing." Many young adults feel somewhat alien to their own Catholic Church. It can be a big, impersonal church with lots of people coming and going. Even in the midst of hundreds of people sitting side-by-side on Sunday, one can feel very alone. As one young adult said, "I walk in on Sunday knowing nobody, and I leave knowing nobody." To be warmly greeted and made to feel that your presence made a difference can be a very important experience.

Some young adults are *shopping around* for a positive experience of the Catholic Church. A good experience of church that begins and ends with warm hellos and handshakes can be much more important than church doctrine and dogma at that moment.

Lastly, hospitality is contagious. It is much more than how a person is welcomed. It affects everyone. It creates a mood and an atmosphere. It communicates spirit.

Planning Young Adult Activities and Events That Work

All church-related group activities fall into four categories: *social, serious, spiritual,* and *service activities.* This is true whether you are planning for a teen group or the "golden-agers." Everything will fit into one of these categories.

Social activities include all that are done purely for enjoyment, including sporting events, theater, parties, etc.

Serious activities include intellectual endeavors like a dialogue group, Bible study, a book club, a speaker series, adult religious education, discussions on current events or politics, etc.

Spiritual activities include young adult Masses, retreats, days of reflection, prayer meetings, etc.

Service activities include any way that the group reaches out to serve, within and outside of the parish.

Every young adult group is different, and what will work best among young adults varies from parish to parish. What works in one parish might fail miserably in a parish just a mile away. It would be foolish to say that there is one activity in each category that is guaranteed to be successful. However, some general guidelines have proven to be true.

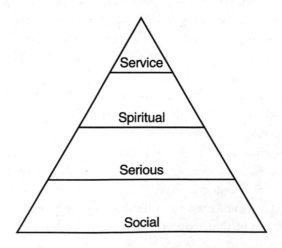

Note the area in each of the four sections of the triangle. In general, the more area in the section, the greater number of young adults you will attract to it. You can usually expect to attract many more young adults for a social event than for a service event. That means that in the early stages of a young adult group, when you are trying to attract new members, hosting a party will be more helpful than inviting people to visit a homeless shelter. It also means that you may have more success with service projects when you link them with social events.

Some young adult groups have been successful staying with one or two categories. In one parish, all the young adults wanted to do was socialize, so they planned one social gathering a month. In the neighboring parish group, the concentration was on spiritual events; they coordinated days of reflection, Masses, retreats, and small faith groups. At one point, the group leaders met and someone joked, "I think we should trade groups for a while. That way, you'll have an opportunity to pray, and we'll get to go out and party!" The groups combined efforts, providing all of their young adults opportunities to do both. More information about collaborative efforts will be provided in the next chapter.

Other young adult groups have made a conscious effort to offer activities in each of the four areas. Especially if you live in an area with a high concentration of young adults, it makes sense to offer a variety of opportunities. Such groups usually have two or three leaders responsible for each area, and offer occasional, well-planned events. If the leaders of each category host three events a year, the calendar will be filled with a strong event each month. Such an approach is likely to reach the greatest number of people, because many young adults choose to participate in only one or two types of events.

In planning effective young adult activities, keep the following strategies in mind:

1. Again, *less is more*. There is a tendency for excited young adult group leaders, fascinated with the possibilities of creating a young adult group, to want to plan a lot of things. Slow down! A few activities done well will be far more effective than a social event every Friday night. If leaders plan a weekly event, who will come? Usually, those people who have no other social life. Is that what is desired? If so, then do it. If you want to attract people who have a social life independent of the young adult group, activities need to be less frequent.

2. *The less required of participants, the greater the response.* Social activities tend to draw greater crowds than do spiritual or service activities. For a social event, little more than attendance is required; for a service event, extra time, talent, and maybe some skill are required. If leaders choose not to have many social activities, they should not ask, "Where is everybody?"

3. *Not everyone is expected to attend everything.* Freedom is one of the hallmarks of the young adult lifestyle. In creating young adult activities, leaders should always let people know they do not *have to* attend everything. A young adult group is not a teen club. Again, no "gottas," no guilt, and no pressure.

4. *Variety is the spice of life.* In developing a young adult group, leaders are encouraged to try activities in each of the four categories. They may not all work, but by trying different things, different people will be attracted, and the group can meet the needs of more people (within and outside itself).

5. *Do the ordinary differently.* This can be a most interesting strategy in planning young adult activities. Once you have gathered names and addresses of all the people you want to participate, personally (in person or by phone, following up with a letter) invite them to a brainstorming session. There are two rules of brainstorming: *anything goes,* and *no criticism.* Begin by writing the word "Social" on a flip chart. Ask, "What social activities might you be interested in attending?" List every response that is generated, and listen carefully for those that seem to generate enthusiasm among those gathered. Continue by asking the same question for the other three categories: serious, spiritual, and service. The list can look rather plain and ordinary. It might resemble a teen club activity list.

Once the list is as complete as possible, ask this question about the items that seemed to generate the most amount of energy: "How do we do that differently?" For example, one of the service activities might be visiting the sick in the parish. That is usually accomplished by visiting the sick parishioners in the local hospital. How do you visit the sick differently? Why not visit them after they are released from the hospital and are recuperating at home? There are usually fewer visitors after hospitalization, fewer people available to help, and perhaps a greater need for visitors to help pass the time, prepare a meal, and make a quick trip to the drug store. The list you generate could set the agenda for the next year!

Here are some examples of creative brainstorming focused on doing the ordinary differently:

Social Activities	
The ordinary	How do you do the ordinary differently?
1. beach volleyball	...in the winter
2. pot luck supper	...complete with foods from family recipes and a story to go with them
— — — — — —	— — — — — —

Serious Activities	
The ordinary	How do you do the ordinary differently?
1. host a speaker series	...obtain videos of significant speakers and host a speaker series "on tape"
2. invite a speaker to your group	...take your group out to "sit at the feet of the master," by going to someone's home or workplace and having an informal discussion
— — — — — —	— — — — — —

Spiritual Activities	
The ordinary	How do you do the ordinary differently?
1. host a weekend retreat	...host a mid-week overnight retreat; or plan a biking/camping retreat over several days
2. young adult Sunday Mass	...as a group, attend Sunday Mass at another church, to hear another preacher or choir, or to worship with people of a different ethnicity or race
— — — — — —	— — — — — —

Service Activities	
The ordinary	How do you do the ordinary differently?
1. visit the sick in the hospital	. . . visit the sick in their homes after hospitalization
2. bring food to the shelter	. . . host a pot luck supper, with everyone preparing an extra dish to bring to the shelter
— — — — — —	— — — — — —

6. *There is a substantial difference between creating a young adult group and hosting young adult activities.* This is important from the very beginning. If leaders set out to develop a parish young adult group, it may have the sound and feel of a "club." The club approach has membership, dues, rules, and an expectation that people participate in almost everything the group plans. That is fine, if that is what you want to create. Another approach is to publicize that the activities offered for young adults through your parish are for any young adults who choose to attend, based on their interests and schedules.

To our list of Principles of Organization, we can now add five more:

#1 With the right people, you can watch the grass grow and have a good time.

#2 The best strategy of invitation is to proceed from the known to the unknown, to move from the most personal to the impersonal.

#3 The Jesus Method of Organizing is most effective. Gather people by direct, personal invitation.

#4 A young adult group is only as good as its leaders.

#5 Less is more: doing a few things well far outweighs doing many things.

#6 Good leadership is gracious, hospitable, and nurtures future leaders.

#7 **Hospitality has four components: before, during, immediately after, and the day after an event.**

#8 **Gracious hospitality means no "gottas," no guilt, no pressure.**

#9   **All church-related group activities fall into four categories: social, serious, spiritual, and service activities. Decide where you want to focus your energy.**

#10 **Do the ordinary differently.**

#11 **There is a substantial difference between creating a young adult group and hosting young adult activities.**

Putting It All Together:
An Organizational Structure for a Young Adult Group

An effective young adult group needs structure to operate smoothly and efficiently. The key to this structure is to *keep it simple*. Every task to be performed does not need a separate committee and many meetings. Additionally, some individuals may perform more than one function.

However, there is a caution here. The leaders must make sure that a select few do not do everything by (and for) themselves. Other young adults must be *invited* to help, and that invitation might have to be extended more than once.

A young adult group should be aware of the following responsibilities:

1. Leadership: All three styles of leadership should be present and functioning well: organizational, popular, and prophetic. You might want to establish a **core group** representing the **three styles of leadership** and varied interest in the **four categories** of activity (social, serious, spiritual, and service). A good way to insure that the various leadership styles and categories of activity are represented is to personally invite people who exhibit those skills into leadership positions.

2. Hospitality: Though hospitality is the responsibility of everyone in leadership positions, at least two young adults with good people skills should oversee the group to assure that hospitality is taking place, *before, during, after, and the day after each event.*

3. Event Planning: For the sake of variety and success, keep in mind the four categories of activities. Host occasional brainstorming sessions with core leaders and young adult participants to keep generating ideas, developing programs, and evaluating past activities. Invite young adults with good leadership skills to assist with the various details of each event. *Keep it simple and keep it fun.*

Young Adult Group Organizational Chart

Use the following chart to name the people who will be responsible for the various positions of the group. Keep in mind that some people may have multiple roles. The chart will help to keep the various responsibilities clear.

CORE GROUP (Primary Leadership Styles)

Organizational leaders: _____

Popular leaders: _____

Prophetic leaders: _____

ACTIVITY COORDINATORS

Social activities: _____

Serious activities: _____

Spiritual activities: _____

Service activities: _____

WORKING TASK FORCES

Hospitality: _____

Event Planning: _____

Outreach: _____

Publicity: _____

Parish Liaison: _____

Finances: _____

4. Outreach: The need for continual outreach to new people and following through with those who participate is an essential part of the organizational structure. Invite two people with good social skills who enjoy contacting and meeting others to watch over this responsibility.

5. Publicity: Keeping young adults, the parish, and the broader community informed about young adult happenings maintains a positive image of the program and assures that its existence and activities are well known. A calendar of events should be printed and sent to all the young adults on your mailing list. Also place it in your own and neighboring parish bulletins, as well as anywhere else young adults gather. If you or others have the resources, communicate via e-mail and the Internet. After an event, write an article presenting the highlights and thanking those who participated and helped to make it happen. Don't forget to add some photos! They do speak louder than words. All this publicity is good public relations, a concrete expression of the purpose and variety of activities of the group.

6. Parish Liaison: It is important that the young adult group stay connected to the life of the parish. It should not become a gathering of younger people off doing their own thing. In order for young adult concerns, interests, and gifts to be understood by the entire parish, one young adult should be a liaison with a parish staff member. Part of the liaison's responsibility is to keep that staff member informed of future goals and upcoming events. The liaison should also invite parish leaders to attend events, even if they come just to greet participants. Ideally, a young adult should also represent the interests of other young adults on the parish council, the parish liturgy committee, and other parish organizations.

The young adult parish liaison can maintain needed dialogue between the parish staff and young adults. The parish staff can learn more about the needs, desires, interests, and spiritual hungers of this elusive age group. Young adults can be kept more aware of parish life and the contributions they can make to it. With this kind of open communication, everyone wins.

A staff member can also encourage participation of young adults in the life of the parish. For example, young adults can be invited to become catechists, liturgical ministers, volunteers, and members of small faith groups.

7. Finances: Someone must be responsible for accounting for money collected and spent, reporting expenses, keeping track of assets, determining costs, and maintaining the financial solvency of the program. Fund-raising efforts fall into this area too.

Every event you host is going to cost money, so from the beginning a financial plan should be developed to promote young adult activities. Most young adult groups begin with a meeting of several young adult leaders and a parish staff member. That meeting is the time to establish what everyone involved is hoping to accomplish and whether or not the parish is able to support the dream of the leaders (at least initially). This support can come in different ways. If the parish is able to provide resources to print and mail information for the first year, as well as the facilities in which to meet, the group can be under way soon. Often the parish is able to pay for refreshments (pop, beer, munchies, and pizza) at initial meetings. Some parishes make a serious commitment to the spirituality and education of young adults by allocating money from their religious education budgets to host a speaker series for them.

However, if money for events is not available in your situation, ask for a suggested donation at each event. Considering the price of a movie today, five dollars to hear an excellent talk on relationships or faith is a bargain.

There is a very simple rule to follow when planning any activity: *Every event must pay for itself.* Remember that young adults *are* adults and are willing to pay for quality opportunities and programs. Before setting the ticket price on any activity, do your best to factor in all related expenses. Consider adding one dollar per person to the cost of every event to cover the cost of future mailings, printing, and other ongoing expenses. After group discounts and donations for various services, even with the extra dollar the ticket price will still be more reasonable than what the same service or event would have cost outside the group.

Keeping in mind that the greatest number of young adults will come to a social event, host an annual fundraising party. Some groups host two fundraisers a year—one to support the group itself and one to raise funds to donate to a worthy cause. Ask businesses in the area to make a contribution of goods or services or to underwrite a speaker stipend. Food donations are graciously accepted, and other donations make attractive raffle prizes. In exchange, provide publicity for the company. To offset the cost of the monthly or quarterly newsletter, consider approaching a local printing company. It may be interested in printing your newsletter in exchange for ad space on the cover. People as a rule want to be generous— but, like volunteers, they need to be asked.

It's Not All Good News:
Eighteen Things That Can Go "Wrong"
in a Young Adult Group, and One Special Concern

Dear Fr. John,

Because of turnover in staff and time, we've put active young adult ministry on hold right now. As I shared with you when we met, our young adult group terminated because of "needy" people. There is no one right now who has the gift, time, and desire to begin again....

Susan

Even with the best leadership and most wonderful activities, young adult groups come and go quickly. An effective young adult group might not last more than two years. That is simply the nature of the age group. Young adults are the most mobile segment of society today and, consequently, of the church. One parish has had four separate young adult groups in twelve years. There are situations when a graceful end to an existing group is in everyone's best interest. When participants leave after making new friends and enjoying a good experience of church, a wonderful goal has been met.

At times our best learning is not from books or theories, but from other people's mistakes. The list below is taken from the experience of young adult groups that we know. It is presented here as a set of issues of which to be aware. If you find your group is losing momentum, you might want to review the list with key leaders and brainstorm possible solutions.

The Lack of Momentum Checklist

1. Lack of clear, strong leadership that is organizational, prophetic, and popular

2. Lack of constant hospitality toward new people

3. Lack of commitment and social responsibility

4. Lack of continued outreach: no new faces

5. Lack of creativity and variety: SOS (same old stuff)

6. Lack of enthusiasm: bad public relations; events that are not fun any longer

7. Lack of needs analysis: leaders only do their thing

8. Lack of the healthy and necessary balance between various personality types: done in by weak or needy people

9. Lack of direct, personal invitation: generic, desperate flyers put everywhere to attract young adults. The conventional form of publicity is generic flyers put in the back of church, inserted into the bulletin, put on cars in the parking lot, and posted on community bulletin boards around town

10. Too narrow: all the same type of activities

11. Too "churchy" ("All we ever do is pray!") or not "church" enough (not spiritually based, just another group)

12. Too small to be effective: low attendance

13. Too single: once they are married, they are gone

14. Too young: often too many irons in the fire

15. Too old: chronologically, that is; the group has lost the ability to attract a balance of the young adult ages (twenties and thirties people) and therefore has lost the ability to regenerate itself

16. Too much work, too little support, too little fun: leader burn out

17. Too much appeal to the "young" in young adult: a semi-teen club

18. Too relevant (all social justice) or not relevant enough (little sense of service, volunteerism, faith, or fun)

If your group is suffering from any of the above, take the time to decide upon some intervention strategies.

A Special Concern: A Mobile Generation

There is another area of concern: **the mobility of young adults.** In addition to being the largest segment of the American population, young adults are also the most mobile part of it. They are mobile in three ways:

1. *Psychic mobility.* Their needs change. This is the time in life when more things of significance are happening for the very first time than have ever happened before or will ever happen again. Young adults are facing life issues, and major decisions need to be made: where to live, what job to pursue, how and where to find a person with whom to spend the rest of their life, whether or not to pursue more education, how to go about

forging adult relationships with family members, how to handle major financial decisions. At any point along the way, an entire life situation can change. The need to meet people greatly diminishes once you have found your significant other or become more settled in a new community. The desire to volunteer changes when you are putting in sixty or more hours a week at work. The drive to buy a place of your own may take precedence over spending money on social events on a regular basis. The availability of time to attend group planning meetings significantly decreases when you decide that more education or skills training is needed and will occupy at least two evenings a week. Once young adults' needs are met or move in a different direction, it is natural for them to leave or be less connected to a young adult group and to move on to the next stage in their lives.

2. *Physical mobility.* Young adults move frequently. Physical mobility encompasses at least four experiences: (*a*) moving into and out of college dorms repeatedly over a period of several years; (*b*) moving from where you grew up to another part of the country; (*c*) moving out of your family home to your own independent living; (*d*) changing addresses frequently within the same area.

It is not uncommon for people, especially those in their twenties, to move every year or two. Jobs, family relationships, educational opportunities, affordable housing, reaching for other goals all can be factors in such moves. Knowing that a good percentage of those who are in a young adult group today will have moved out of the area by this time next year—including the leaders—helps to stay ahead of the situation. Expect people to move. Because people move the continual invitation to new people is essential. So is training new leaders. If the group can continue drawing new members, it will survive and be helpful to young adults who choose to participate. In such a highly mobile society, without new young adults participating in the group the odds of its survival for more than a year or two are very low.

3. *Relational mobility.* Significant friendships are made and broken often among young adults. Remember that one of the strongest needs of young adults is to meet people, make friends, and establish some very important relationships. So much of young adulthood is based on getting connected to others. It is only natural that in a young adult group that does a good job introducing people to one another, deeper relationships form. When

two people fall in love and are considering marriage, they may not stay connected to the group. The time they gave to the group's activities is now given almost exclusively to each other. Such relationships take time and attention. That's fine. If some component or activity of the group is helpful to them in the future, they will return. Keep in mind that an effective young adult group is for people in their twenties and thirties, both married and single.

A difficult situation regarding relational mobility occurs when two people in the group who have become close friends end that relationship. Very often it becomes uncomfortable for either or both to participate in the group's activities. One or both might choose to leave the group. This is not a reflection on the group as much as it is a relational decision. Respect that decision. Unless told otherwise, keep both people informed about future activities.

Any young adult group will have a constant flow of members into and out of it. This is no cause for guilt. People must know that they are free to come and go as they want and need to do so. Being respectful of where people are in their lives is another important part of hospitality. If they have good memories of their time with your group, you have made a significant difference.

To Summarize...

Steps for forming a parish young adult group:

1. Gather several young adults and meet with a parish staff member to discuss possibilities.

2. Develop a profile of who you want to participate.

3. Create a list of names of people who fit your profile:

    (a) List the names of those who are known personally

    (b) Add names from the parish census forms

    (c) Add names from school and religious education lists

    (d) Add names of anyone else people know who fit the profile

    (e) Collect names through the parish bulletin

(f) Collect names through announcements in places that young adults frequent

(g) Collect names through local newspapers and other newsletters

4. At the brainstorming session, invite members of the group to sign in, meet one another, and brainstorm activities of interest in each of the four categories (social, serious, spiritual, service). Then, work your way through that list a second time, brainstorming ideas for doing the ordinary differently. Have a core leader keep track of which events elicit the most enthusiasm and of anyone who offers to help in any way. Distribute volunteer sign-up pages, so that you have a record of all who want to help and the gifts they have to share.

5. The core leaders should then meet again to use the wisdom of the brainstorming session to decide upon a future direction.

We can now complete our list of Principles of Organization:

#1 With the right people, you can watch the grass grow and have a good time.

#2 The best strategy of invitation is to proceed from the known to the unknown, to move from the most personal to the impersonal.

#3 The Jesus Method of Organizing is most effective. Gather people by direct, personal invitation.

#4 A young adult group is only as good as its leaders.

#5 Less is more: doing a few things well far outweighs doing many things.

#6 Good leadership is gracious, hospitable, and nurtures future leaders.

#7 Hospitality has four components: before, during, immediately after, and the day after an event.

#8 Gracious hospitality means no "gottas," no guilt, no pressure.

#9 All church-related group activities fall into four categories: social, serious, spiritual, and service activities. Decide where you want to focus your energy.

#10 Do the ordinary differently.

#11 There is a substantial difference between creating a young adult
     group and hosting young adult activities. Hosting young adult ac-
     tivities fits their lifestyle.

#12 **The continual invitation of new people to young adult activities
     and leadership positions keeps the group alive, young adult, and
     exciting.**

Now take the information from this chapter, and apply it to your situation.
What might a young adult group look like, based on your dream and your
parish? Who are some key people who can help you implement the strategy
presented here? Jump back to the beginning of this chapter, and establish
your first steps.

Chapter 6

Especially for Parish Pastoral Ministers...

Celebrating Moments of Return

Contrary to what many people believe, there is not a massive exodus of young adults from the Catholic Church. As a matter of fact, Catholics have one of the lowest attrition rates of any religious group in America. Young adults state that they are Catholic. They have been baptized into the faith and continue to express an identity with the faith. But that is just not good enough for many church ministers today. *Registration* in a parish sometimes takes precedence over *membership* in the Catholic Church. Just ask young adults the first question they, their peers, siblings, or Catholic friends are asked when they approach the church to celebrate a marriage or baptize a child. "Are you registered?" If the answer is no, the availability of those sacraments diminishes quickly and dramatically. "I called five churches today looking for a place to be married," one young adult reported. "Every one asked if I was registered. Not one asked if I was Catholic! No one ever bothered to ask if I was in love!"

Today church ministers speak a great deal about evangelization. Perhaps it is time we learn that the first moments of adult faith for many people are marriage and passing on the faith to the next generation. A warm, sincere, compassionate welcome at the time of marriage will do more to nurture an adult relationship with the church than "I'm sorry. We only marry registered parishioners."

We continue to teach that a sacramental moment does not end something; it begins something. Let a life of marriage in the Lord also begin an adult relationship with the local church by choice, not end that possibility by default. If forced to, young adults will register. They will attend all

65

compulsory preparation programs. They will do it our way. They, also, will not forget. Most will continue to put a check mark in that Catholic box on the survey form. Yet when the "assembly" gathers to be in communion with one another and the Lord, many young adults will not feel in union with that assembly.

Perhaps the pastoral strategy needed here is to learn how to *celebrate* their moments of return. Young adults' moments of return are not limited to a return to the church after time away. There are also moments of return to the depth of life that occur in very special and often intense moments, for example, marriage and baptism. There are at least three more such moments in the young adult years of life—moments of sickness, death, and personal decision.

Life can be unfair. For young adults the unfairness and unevenness of life is seen in the sickness and disease they experience themselves and witness among family members and friends. These are profoundly spiritual moments when hard questions and profound realities need to be addressed.

The same is true for moments of death. The experience of death becomes real for many during the young adult years. The death of close family members or friends calls young adults more deeply into the mystery of life. Moments of death are profoundly sacred.

Though less visible than marriage or baptism and less dramatic than sickness or death, moments of personal decision are nonetheless important. This generation will change jobs five or six times. Decisions about relationships, dating, and marriage are complex and are not entered into lightly. They are moments of meaning and personal identity. These moments, too, open many young adults to the spiritual side of their lives.

All these moments (and many more) can be nurtured and celebrated not just by young adults' relationship to the church, but, maybe more importantly, by the church's relationship to them. That relationship can be developed in at least four ways: (1) stressing compassion before legalism, (2) adopting the Jesus Method of Organizing, (3) developing the "third moment" of sacraments, (4) living the Catholic tradition as a spiritual path.

1. *Compassion before legalism* reflects the attitude of Christ. He loved and embraced people who didn't always do it right. Can we do the same, especially with people who do not always understand church laws and local parish customs? Perhaps they need to know they are wanted, appreciated,

and accepted as members of the church, the Body of Christ, first and foremost. Once you know you belong, you are much more open with regard to *how* to belong.

We all know how it feels to be treated kindly instead of rudely, to be helped instead of frustrated, to be supported rather than abandoned, and to be embraced rather than rejected. We should always respond with graciousness, patience, and compassion. When it is necessary to invoke the rules, we should do so by explaining each one experientially, honestly, and pastorally.

2. *The Jesus Method of Organizing* (see above p. 41) is a positive response to the critique that young adults are just not around the parish and that they never volunteer for anything. If they are personally contacted and invited to attend, there is a greater chance they will. If they are personally contacted and asked to help, there is a greater chance they will do that too. Graciously and personally we can invite young adults to participate in church life. Jesus used that strategy when he invited the apostles, one by one, to walk with him.

This is also the most direct and effective way to move young adults who are affiliate Catholics to become more practicing ones. We need to get the word out to this elusive group of people—who often don't believe that there is anything really for them in the local church—that we do care and we do have opportunities that might respond to their questions and concerns.

When young adults attend weekend Mass, do they see any of their peers as ushers, communion ministers, lectors, or choir members? If they do not, and you as a minister want them to, then try the Jesus Method. Use direct personal invitation. It worked for the one we call Lord and Savior, and it can work for those in pastoral, liturgical, or catechetical ministry today.

3. *The third moment of a sacrament* provides another pastoral strategy for the local church in developing a relationship with young adult people. As we said above, the sacraments of marriage and the baptism of their children for many young adults mark the beginning of their adult relationship with the church. An effective ministry to young adults can be built around their participation in those sacraments. The sacraments of marriage and baptism have three distinct moments: preparation, celebration, and follow-up.

A great deal of time and planning has gone into developing the first

Parish outreach teams

One pastor mentioned that he rarely sees the young couples whose children he baptizes at Sunday Mass or at any parish activity. Such parishes might develop "Parish Outreach Teams," whose only ministry would be to stay in contact with younger singles, couples, and families. It would be simple outreach. The young adults would not have to attend anything. It would be the local church stopping by once in a while or people on the outreach team calling just to say "hello" and stay in contact—an unexpected form of hospitality for a Catholic parish!

two moments of these sacraments. It is time to concentrate on the third moment, namely, the five years immediately following the marriage of young adults or the baptism of their child. This is an ideal time for the parish to enter into a relationship with these young couples or young families.

Follow-up and an ongoing relationship with the newly married couple or young adult family should be an essential part of ministry. In this third moment the local church, its ministers and people, reach out with missionary zeal to its own young adults. It involves supporting their marriages, inquiring about their family, and demonstrating on a regular basis, in person or by phone, a genuine interest in and care for them as God's people.

When we call people now, it is usually for a donation, because we want them to volunteer, or because they have not done something (gone to church, enrolled their child in CCD, paid tuition, etc.). Instead, we can just enter into communion with them. It is going to take a year or two. Call them whether they go to church or not. Let them know you are interested in how they are. Keep it personal. A letter in the mail will not do what a phone call can do. You want interaction. Direct, personal contact makes all the difference. Young families are asking lots of good questions. "My child is three years old. How should we be praying?" We can address some of that. If you talk to someone long enough, you are going to hear about that person's life and needs. You can bring the information back to the parish staff and ask, "What can we do about this?" Chances are you will begin to hear about things more than once. Follow the principle of convergence: questions that are repeated will start to form a trend, and you have the opportunity to do something about finding solutions.

Here is one way of making the third moment of the sacrament of baptism an effective ministerial tool in the parish. Designate some key younger couples as the parish's liaisons to people who have had their children baptized recently. A designated couple calls each family four times a year for the next five years. Their task is simple: ask, "How are you?" They genuinely are reaching out in the name of the parish and inquiring about the well-being of the young family. Needless to say, this will be very awkward for the first year or two. Not many people receive phone calls from their church because someone is concerned about their well-being. But that is the mission of the church—to reach out to others and to exhibit care for them.

There are certain questions the designated couple should not ask, such as, "Are you going to church?" "How often are you going to church?" and "Are you supporting the parish?" The purpose of the phone calls is not interrogation, but a simple, genuine interest in learning, "How are you?" The goal is to establish a relationship between one couple calling in the name of the church and another couple who are a part of that church. After several years, the designated couple might begin to learn about some of the needs and concerns of this couple and their family. They might begin to discover the couple's relationship to the Catholic Church and what they might need from the church at this time in their lives.

The designated couples should share with the parish staff some of the findings from these phone calls. Toward the end of the five-year telephone process, there is a good chance that the needs and wants expressed by this young family might assist the parish in its continual development of programs and activities.

Here is another possibility for the third moment of the sacrament of marriage. Ask couples to provide their permanent addresses after marriage. Send out an invitation once a year to everyone who has been married at your parish to attend a liturgy and a party. It is not only for those who worship at your parish or who are members there. It is for those who have been married there over the past year. The church where people are married is a significant religious symbol in their lives. They might have moved, but to be invited back to the place where they celebrated a sacrament is very important. They come back. Do it on the Saturday closest to Valentine's Day to make it more romantic. The "mission" is to marriage, not to members. Part of the mission of any parish that works with young adults is to marry people. Invite people to the third moment of the sacrament of their wedding—to return to that sacred space where it happened and celebrate it again.

This is very different from worrying about emptying out the parking lot for the next crowd. We are so large that we have limited ourselves to what we can do in an hour and fifteen minutes. Because we have so many people coming and going, our hospitality has become shallow, and we can't get to know everyone's name. Young adults are looking for personal contact. This third moment of the sacrament is a way of staying personally connected and going out to them without asking for anything in return. Jesus went from town to town. He did not stand in one place and wait for people to come to him. Good Christianity is mission driven. We talk about it in areas of social justice and building a better world and moving out among the poor and witnessing. Why can't we apply those principles of community and connectedness in our parishes? There is a priest we know who, during the first five years of his assignment, personally visited every parishioner. That is unheard of, but it makes an incredible difference.

4. *Offering our Catholic tradition as a spiritual path to follow throughout life* is a fourth way to develop the church's relationship with young adults. The most frequently used spiritual program in America today is the Twelve Step Program. Consider step five: "Admit to God, to ourselves, and to another human being the exact nature of our wrongs." It sounds like Catholic confession. Young adults often ask: "Why do I have to go to confession?" and "Why do I have to confess to a priest?" Helping young adults seek a spiritual path might mean helping them ask the right questions. The right questions are those generated by the lived experiences of all people, not by a detail or ritual of a particular religion: How do I get free from my past? How do I stay free to be faithful? Once those questions are asked, we can offer any searcher or seeker a variety of spiritual paths, rooted in the Catholic tradition, that lead to freedom, for example, a better understanding of the Penitential Rite at the beginning of Mass, participation in a liturgical reconciliation service, a regular examination of conscience, and participation in the Sacrament of Reconciliation.

In a world of advertising that says, "You're as good as you feel," many young adults don't feel good. They can look good on the outside. Fashion, clothes, and glamour can take care of that. But on the inside, where life really matters, they want to know if anyone cares if they are around. The search for meaning is often a search for other people of meaning: "With whom can I share life?" "Are there people around who share my values?" "How do you meet good people once you've moved to a new location?"

Young adults are looking for connection. They are searching for communion. At Catholic Mass, we literally hold out that communion. "The Body of Christ," we say to them. "Amen" is what we hope to hear in response. Communion can be Bread for that spiritual hunger. Even more than a moment of personal piety or private religious expression, it is a communal moment. Eucharist is a sacred communal moment that says: you are an important member of this Body of Christ, and at this table there is always room for you. When we are together, when we are in communion with one another, when we fill another place at the Table of the Lord with your presence, then we are on the path to glory.

We might not be able to make life easier for young adult people. Struggles, broken dreams, disappointments are a part of the human landscape for us all. But we can share them and together let the richness of our Catholic faith give them meaning. By doing so, those of us who minister in the church today can reveal the sacramentality that drives our tradition. By our actions and our words, we can enter into communion with young adults. We can teach them where God dwells—in every moment of life, in the good times and bad, in sickness and health, in the times alone and the times with others. All of them are shared with a God who loves us.

Preaching

If we could do only one thing in our drive to revitalize our local churches, that should be to develop the skill of preaching. Young adults critique Sunday Mass through the lens of preaching more than any other way. You will not hear many of them talk about the processional cross, how many candles were on the altar, whether or not the priest or deacon was wearing a symbolically meaningful stole, or if white wine or red was placed on the altar of the Lord. They will, however, comment, loudly and often, about preaching. Preaching the Word of the Lord is an extremely important

Photo by Stephen Serio

Cardinal Joseph Bernardin, during his homily at the Theology-on-Tap Mass in 1985, said, "If I had children of my own, they would be your age. You are special to me and to the church in our archdiocese."

means to connect the Gospel of Jesus Christ with their work, their world, their families, and their beliefs.

Why not have an annual preaching workshop as part of expected on-going training sessions for bishops, priests, deacons, and lay preachers? All professionals and skilled trades people must keep up. Most have mandatory sessions on how to do their work better.

It has always been the few, not the many, who have been involved in parish life. The overwhelming majority of Catholics will attend church on Sunday and come to the church for sacred moments in their life: birth, death, marriage, sickness, communion, confirmation. Critical to those moments is good worship and good preaching. In a world in which we are bombarded by nonstop words from radio and television, preaching is more important now than ever. Here is what some young adults had to say about preaching:

> *I see the following as not currently in place in many of our parishes: quality liturgy, complete with good music, excellent hospitality, and thought-provoking preaching.*

Why are thousands of people going out to Barrington every Sunday for a worship service that resembles a tent meeting? Why do Jimmy Swaggart and Rex Humbard still draw a crowd? Why does Robert Schuler have that fabulous cathedral in California? Because those guys can preach one helluva sermon. Maybe the seminaries need to emphasize sermon giving more. Draw the people in with good sermons and they'll keep coming back. Line up a couple more good sermon givers for the future.

Relate the Gospel and reading to everyday life and how we can and should pass our goodness (God's Spirit) on to others. Relating the Scriptures to current events is also very effective.

I believe that the main reason young adults go to church is that they find the sermon interesting, enlightening, uplifting, or something along these lines. Therefore, it would be valuable to suggest that priests think hard about how half of their audience (women) will hear the sermon. Does the sermon implicitly assume that everyone is male or everyone's experience was as a male?

Homilies can be a place to explain symbolism, not plead poverty.

Find a parish without a school. Turn it into a young adult parish. Staff it with dynamic, secularly savvy priests. Teach them how to give better homilies, focused on life issues. Give a reason to be there.

Be creative in your ideas. What about a sermon that's a dialogue between parishioners and priest? Don't be afraid to break the mold.

Chapter 7

Connecting Collegians

Recently a bishop vesting for a confirmation ceremony received this unsolicited piece of advice from a parish youth minister. "Bishop, I want to suggest a new ritual for you to use at the end of the confirmation liturgy today. Invite forward one more time all those who have been confirmed, and give each one a kiss good-bye."

Although there is no indication that our young people are leaving the Catholic Church, it is apparent that after confirmation many of them are less present and active in the life of the parish.

This seems to be occurring no matter the age or level of education at which young people participate in the sacrament of confirmation, and no matter what type of religious formation and practice has preceded the sacramental liturgy. For many the time of return to a more active practice of the faith is at the next sacrament, marriage. But considering the age at which many people choose to marry today, the "time between sacraments" is getting longer and longer. The longer the time that young adults live without contact, exposure, or practice of the faith, the less apparent need there is for it.

However, the time between sacraments, the early young adult years, is very important. Events of significance and substance—eye-opening education, career choices, marriage, the birth of children—often are experienced by people in their twenties. And such events are "religious" moments. Human moments of love, brokenness, birth, sickness, and possibility are the drama of life, and each of these moments is filled with both the quest for meaning and the presence of God.

It is important that these years between sacraments be times that the local parish *reaches out* to its young adult people, constantly *invites* their presence, *welcomes* their participation, and *calls* them to live Gospel values in their lives. It is time for the church to go out to them and not simply wait for them to ring the parish house bell when it's time for the next sacrament.

For many people these are the college years. And for some that means attending a school away from home. What follows are suggested ways the local parish can stay in touch with people who are now living in the time between sacraments and make the college years important years of church identity.

The Big Send-Off

By mid-August young people begin to return to college. We know of several parishes that have sent their college students off to school just as religious congregations send their members off to a mission. College students are on a mission to learn, to develop, and to live out their values. At weekend Masses, after the homily those leaving for college are invited to stand in place or come forward into the sanctuary. The presider of the liturgy gives them the "call" to go forth from their parish with the blessing of family, friends, and the parish family of God to a new year of educational formation. They are called to take with them the dreams, hopes, and vision that God has for the world and for each of them.

These young adults can be invited to say aloud their names and the colleges they will be attending. As a sign of support, all present at Mass are invited to extend outstretched arms and hands toward those who are college-bound and, by reading together a printed blessing and prayer, share the hopes and dreams of the parish for their well-being.

Don't Forget to Write

The parish can designate several people (perhaps parents of those away at school) as liaisons to the parishioners away at college. During the last several weeks in August and the first few weeks of September, a simple bulletin announcement can be prepared, asking parents to send to the rectory the mailing addresses of their college students. The liaison committee can then mail the weekly parish bulletin to the students.

On occasion, a personal letter or the announcement of special parish activities can be included with the weekly bulletin: Thanksgiving Day

Invite the parents

Invite the parents of college students to join the committee that helps the parish stay in contact with them. They have a strong interest in maintaining contact between their sons and daughters and the Catholic Church. Let the parents help these young adults know how much their parish cares for them. Invite parishioners who are alumni of a particular college or university to visit students from their parish who are at their school. They will enjoy visiting and praying in the place they worshiped at an earlier time. Everyone benefits!

Mass times, parish Christmas events, Lenten practices during spring break, Holy Week activities, and special programs for college students. A college mailing list can be included one week with the bulletin, indicating where other college parishioners are living and attending school.

A weekly piece of mail, not just from home but a reminder of thoughtfulness from the parish itself, can have greater impact than even college students will admit. College years can be wonderful but difficult years. They are times of decision making, the testing of values, and dealing with family expectations. These are the years when kids become adults, actions become habits (some of which are virtues), and mistakes lead to insights. A consistent outreach by the local parish might never be forgotten. More than one college graduate has told us, "When I was away at school, like clockwork, each week my parish remembered me with the bulletin. Sometimes they even surprised me with what I would find inside the envelope!"

Take the Parish to the Parishioners

A mailing list of college parishioners will quickly tell a liaison committee and parish staff which colleges most parishioners attend. Interestingly, most will not be more than several hours from home. Most will probably be in state schools. Some parish staff members have traveled to the schools to visit their college parishioners.

Here's how a college visit can take place. A special letter can be sent to all parishioners at any given school. It can be sent to them in a special mailing or included with the weekly bulletin mailing.

The agenda for a college visit is simple. People gather at a set time at the campus ministry center. A special Mass or worship service can be celebrated. After that, it's out for dinner with the "parishioners." Bring a camera—these historical events should be recorded. The photographs and names of college parishioners pictured can be printed in the Sunday bulletin. How proud parents are to see pictures of their college kids at school—and at church while at school! And, although they might not say so, how proud those young adults are of their parish, that it thinks enough of them to visit them while "away" at school. That is evangelization, pure and simple. Follow it up with a thank-you note from the parish staff visitors to the college students who took the time to pray and socialize.

Put Out the Welcome Mat

Christmas vacation is an ideal time to gather those who have been away at school. Some parishes have hosted a welcome home party in the rectory or parish house. The rectory is an important building for Catholics. It is where parishioners meet with staff before sacramental moments, where some people go for counseling, and where the priests live. Anyone can have a party in the church hall, but to have a party in the rectory has an aura of specialness attached to it. That's the point. For college-aged young adults, this time between sacraments needs special care and treatment. They need to be told in many ways just how important they are to the church. To welcome them home with a party in their honor hosted by the parish staff in the rectory says a lot.

A Summertime Special: Theology-on-Tap

Theology-on-Tap, which will be described in greater detail in chapter 11 (see p. 140), began as a program to assist young adults with the larger issues of life. It has become a forum that allows the Catholic tradition to speak on an adult level to young adults. Theology-on-Tap begins the week after the Fourth of July and concludes four weeks later, before most people return to college. There is a shared understanding among many church

A word to college campus ministers...

Many colleges have excellent Catholic student centers and fine young people participating in the life of the church there. It is important to continue the participation of these young people in the church when they are home on vacation or returning home upon the completion of their academic programs. Contact the home parishes of your students and inform them of the type of ministries in which the students have been involved. Encourage the parish to personally invite these young people to continue their ministries at home. Most if not all of the students and graduates would be honored to be invited to continue in those leadership positions. It's another way of letting them know how important they are to the parish.

ministers that summer is not a good time to conduct church programs. This is simply not the case. It depends on *when* during the summer a program is offered. After the Fourth of July, people actually look for things to do and places to go. Earlier in the summer, young adults can be very busy seeing who's home, getting into a summertime job routine, and attending this concert and that picnic. After a while, they actually have time to spare. Theology-on-Tap not only fills some of that time, but also has become a significant religious formation program for young adults.

A Summer Young Adult Mass

When we think of youth or young adult Masses, we tend to think of a special liturgy at a special time in a special place. If young adults are a parish priority, the parish should consider shaping one of its weekend Masses with a young adult focus. This can be accomplished with three minor adjustments:

1. placing young adults in the liturgical roles of lectors, communion ministers, ushers/greeters, and cantors;

2. shaping the preaching to speak to young adults and their world of experiences;

3. using music that is familiar to the age group.

Otherwise, it is a parish weekend Mass that everyone in the parish is free to attend. One parish that offered a special summer young adult Mass at 10:30 a.m. soon discovered that it had become the best attended weekend Mass.

The overused word "evangelization" usually means developing a strategy that offers healing to those hurt by the church or a welcome to those who experience alienation from the church. It's time to get very serious about evangelization to those who haven't yet had time to be hurt or alienated. Many of them are just missing-in-action. The time we wait for young adults to come to us, the next sacramental time, is becoming longer and longer. It's time for us to go to them.

PART THREE

BEYOND THE PARISH

Chapter 8

Regional Young Adult Ministry

The concept of a ministerial outreach beyond a single parish is not new. It is part of an old and effective strategy in our Catholic history. As mentioned earlier, even when our Catholic parishes were thriving, they could not do it all. New movements, organizations, and ministries were created and grew to meet human and spiritual needs. New forms of Catholic expression and identity worked before. We can repeat that historical success.

Many people are not parish-based Catholics at this time in their lives. But they are still Catholic. Parishes can join together to create a common young adult ministry for the good of the church. Such an outreach is both pastorally and economically sound. Some parishes, no matter how hard they try, can find only a few young adults interested in joining a young adult group or participating in young adult activities. When a group of parishes work together to help these people participate in church life, the numbers increase. Being in a room filled with your peers who share your values generates energy. As young people meet and talk with each other, they begin to realize that they are not alone in their questions and search for meaning.

Not every parish is capable of responding to the needs of every group. Combining resources makes sense and takes the pressure off each individual parish. Very few parishes can afford to pay the salary of a young adult minister. But when several parishes contribute toward the office and salary, each has the benefit of another full-time staff member for a fraction of the cost.

To begin an areawide young adult ministry, a group of parishes should hire a young adult minister to work with all the parishes' young adults. Difficulties arise when parish leaders become territorial or fail to stay connected and supportive. As a church we are not used to this much collaboration. Parish leaders must support this effort wholeheartedly and not be worried about one parish robbing another parish of its young adults. If that negative line of reasoning takes hold, the areawide outreach will not work. If the regional young adult minister feels unsupported, again, the efforts will fail. Each parish must name a staff person to support and work with the area young adult minister.

With an areawide outreach, the needs of young adults can be more easily met. The possibility of gathering larger groups of people can become a reality, which will increase the likelihood of long-term success. The cost of the outreach will be much less than that of a parish young adult minister, and the ministry will have many more resources at its disposal (meeting and event space, staff contacts, phone lines, etc.).

The Mission of a Regional Young Adult Minister

The mission of a regional young adult minister is fourfold:

- to establish contacts and working relationships with each participating parish;

- to gather names and compile a list of young adults in their twenties and thirties, married and single, in participating parishes;

- to establish an outreach to young adults in their twenties and thirties, married and single, in participating parishes;

- to respond to the expressed needs of young adults in participating parishes.

Below are specific tasks to be accomplished for each component of this mission.

To establish contacts and working relationships with each participating parish.

1. Select a ministerial staff person in each parish who has an interest in young adults. These are the people with whom the young adult minister will be in direct contact for information about events and activities in the participating parishes. These staff people will help develop parish contacts

with young adults. They will be the ones to whom the young adult minister reports on activities and results of the areawide outreach.

2. Select two to four young adults from each parish with whom to begin developing an areawide ministry. Known by the parish staff to be leaders, these individuals, married and single, will be the foundation for gathering an effective group of young adults both in their parish and in the neighboring parishes.

3. Select several parents of young adults in each parish to work in conjunction with the young adult minister. The parents are needed to establish a network among other parents both to encourage and invite their young adult children into church participation. Besides being an influence in their parish and in the lives of their adult children, parents also speak clearly about the needs of their family, especially their young adult children. The parents can assist with funding, advocacy, and other forms of support (services, equipment, and products) needed to make a regional young adult ministry operate smoothly and creatively.

4. Create a list of chaplains and pastoral counselors to be used in the ministry. Everyone has different gifts and skills. From the very beginning of the mission, the young adult minister needs to know what resources are available. Who are the gifted preachers, catechists, liturgical presiders, pastoral counselors, marriage and interpersonal counselors who can be used directly or on a referral basis by the young adult minister and by young adults in the area?

5. Compile an inventory of all activities in each participating parish. This inventory would include the type of people who participate (age, lifestyle, numbers), the frequency of meetings, the requirements for involvement, and the names, addresses, phone numbers, and e-mail addresses of the leaders and contact people. The inventory is valuable for directing young adults to existing activities from which they might benefit.

To gather names and compile a list of young adults in their twenties and thirties, married and single, in participating parishes.

1. Solicit from each parish the names, addresses, and phone numbers of young adults found on the parish database. This will include young adults who have registered on their own and those who were registered as part of their parents' family unit.

2. Ask parish staff personnel to identify the young adults they know

personally. This list will include young adults involved in liturgical functions, catechists, friends, former youth group participants, newly married couples, those who have recently had a child baptized, etc.

3. Publish a series of bulletin announcements for consecutive weeks soliciting the names of young adults. The response will generate a list of interested young adults who have taken the initiative to respond but who are not necessarily registered in the parish.

4. Make a brief announcement at all the weekend Masses in each parish to introduce the regional young adult ministry and solicit the names (and help) of young adults in this effort. Reference could be made to a young adult registration card found in the pews or printed in the parish bulletin. The regional young adult minister can be present after each Mass to collect the registration cards, make personal contacts, and answer questions.

5. Publish articles in the local community newspapers about the program and invite people to send in the names of young adults to the regional young adult minister.

6. Post an announcement flyer soliciting names at places where young adults gather: laundromats, convenience stores, bars, train stations, etc.

7. Develop and maintain a database of young adults from each parish in the area. This database would code information about each person, such as parish affiliation, marital status, special needs (divorced, parent, Twelve Step), special interests (Bible, sports), skills (writer, musician, photographer), and lifestyle (working, college).

To establish an outreach to young adults in their twenties and thirties, married and single, in participating parishes.

1. Compose a letter of introduction to the ministry that will be mailed to all young adults in the regional database. This letter will introduce the young adult minister as well as the program. It will clearly describe the purpose with examples of activities (social, serious, spiritual, service, see above p. 50). It can solicit special concerns from young adults (young marrieds, singles, charismatics, athletes, divorced, etc.). This introductory letter might include two inserts: an activity preference page and a name/address page of other young adults to be added to the database.

2. Schedule personal interviews with young adults. There is no substitute for personal attention. Personal interviews are the best way to build serious bonds between young adults, the young adult minister, the

On these sample registration cards we ask for date of birth. This helps to target our mailings and our ministry to young adults.

Sample Registration Card #1

Please keep me informed about Young Adult Ministry!

Name: _____

Address: _____

City: _____ State: ____ Zip: _____

Home phone: _____ Work phone: _____

Date of birth: _____ E-mail: _____

☐ Please add my name to the Young Adult Ministry Office mailing list.

☐ My e-mail address is listed above. Please send me your monthly e-letter.

☐ I'm interested in volunteering in the Young Adult Ministry Office.

Is there anything else we can do for you? Please explain.

Sample Registration Card #2

An invitation to get connected to
Young Adult Ministry

Young adult ministry is the outreach of our Catholic Church to women and men, single and married, in their twenties and thirties. If you are a young adult, or the parent or friend of young adults, we invite you to send their names and addresses to us. We will keep them informed of opportunities to gather with their peers. You can reach us by phone (. . .), e-mail (. . .), fax (. . .), or mail (Young Adult Ministry, . . .).

Name: _____

Address: _____

City: _____ State: ____ Zip: _____

Home phone: _____ Work phone: _____

Date of birth: _____ E-mail: _____

Catholic Church, and the regional outreach to them. More data and information are gathered in an interview than from a written survey form. Make sure that you select the young adults to be interviewed randomly. This will insure the best cross-section of data; it will also insure that active and nonactive, churched and nonchurched young adults are interviewed.

3. Follow up each personal interview with a letter, a phone call, or some other appropriate action. A simple written note of thanks in most instances is sufficient. However, some interviews might reveal a need that the young adult minister can respond to with other appropriate actions. For example, if a young adult expresses an interest in music, the young adult minister can contact the parish music directors and have them establish contact with the young adult.

4. Interview other young adults by telephone. Telephone interviews allow more young adults to be contacted. Though not as personal as face-to-face interviews, phone outreach still allows for direct contact and the opportunity for conversation. Again, conversation can surface more needs, feedback, and ideas than a written survey. Follow up with thank-you notes.

5. Arrange meetings between the young adult minister and small groups of ten to twelve young adults. This maintains the value of personal contact and provides the opportunity of reaching more people to explore their concerns. The minister can get their feedback and reactions to the proposed outreach to them and their peers. The small groups are also face-to-face opportunities for people to meet one another and see who else is interested in issues of church and faith.

6. Complete a postinterview form for each young adult contacted. After each personal, phone, or group interview, the young adult minister should record reactions and pertinent comments. It is important to insure that people and their ideas do not get lost, misplaced, or forgotten. Often new ideas or variations on existing ideas will surface. Writing them down immediately will help establish a catalog of suggestions, strategies, and resources. A written postinterview form can also serve as an inventory of the talents and skills of the young adults that might enhance both the areawide project and the work and ministry of the individual parishes.

7. Submit a report about these interviews to staff members and the governance boards of the participating parishes. Because this is a regional ministry, accountability is extremely important. A written report detailing the number of young adults interviewed, their comments and

reactions about the church and parish life, their specific articulated needs and reaction to the project should be submitted to all levels of the parish leadership: the deans, pastors, staffs, councils, and advisory boards. The young adult minister is not simply developing another church program but is also obtaining feedback from an entire generation of Catholics about church life as young adults see it.

To respond to the expressed needs of young adults in participating parishes.

1. Direct young adults to programs, activities, and parishes that have outlets for their expressed needs. Many effective parish programs and activities are already in place. There is no need to begin something new every time several people have an idea or express a need. Sometimes they simply have to be directed to what is currently available. Unless there is a good reason not to do so (for example, if everyone in the existing program is more than twice their age), do not hesitate to direct young adults to what already exists. Integration into parish life is often what the young adults need. The strategy here is a cluster model, not a parish model. Young adults will travel to find what they seek, and every program does not have to happen in every parish.

2. Contact the leaders of parish programs in the area and share with them the names, addresses, and phone numbers of the young adults who have expressed an interest in what they offer. Using the inventory of parish programs and contact people, the young adult minister can contact the leaders with the names of young adults, information about them, and the need they expressed. The program leaders can then contact the young adults to invite their participation and answer any questions.

3. Connect with young adults frequently: on one-month, three-month or six-month intervals, depending on what they are seeking. This will determine if they have become connected, if the activity responds to their need, or if there might be a better option. It will also show that the church is taking a personal interest in them. That interest and follow-up might be more important than the programs offered.

4. Follow up with the program leaders to insure that they have contacted the interested young adults. It is important to inquire about the presence, interest, and level of activity of the young adults. It is just as important to make sure that program leaders follow through. Too many

young adults justifiably feel that they fall through the cracks of parish programs.

5. When needed, develop programs that are similar to existing parish programs but that are tailored to young adults. One example is a support group for young adults who have been divorced. Though such support groups exist in many parishes, often they attract few younger people. A similar case can be made for marriage enrichment programs. A group of parishes could create an activity designed to explore and support the early years of marriage, which are usually the young adult years.

6. Develop programs and activities specifically designed around the expressed needs of young adults. As with any age group of Catholics, there are needs specific to young adults. The greatest need among any group is for social events. People want to gather socially with peers under the auspices of the church. Social activities will always attract the most people. They allow people to meet one another and begin to develop community. But effective young adult ministry does not stop there. There are three other areas of young adult life that can lead to very effective church programming: relationships, faith, and work. To address these concerns the other categories of activities (serious, spiritual, and service) need to be developed. Offer a variety of opportunities that will address the needs and interests of young adults.

The Tasks of a Regional Young Adult Ministry

If you are interested in creating an areawide outreach to young adults, take a good look at the tasks listed below. Let them guide your planning, but only you can determine what will work best in your situation.

1. Determine **which parishes in your area are interested** in participating, and have a good conversation with their leadership about the possibility. Reach for a two-year commitment. The first year will be spent building relationships and dreaming. The second year is when you will see some good results. The number of parishes to be included will depend upon the number of young adults in the area, the financial resources available, the level of commitment each parish is willing to accept, and the geographic territory to be covered. An areawide ministry can be successful with as few as two parishes and as many as eight. If your diocese has a Young Adult Ministry Office, it can be helpful in presenting the idea of a

regional young adult ministry to staff members they know to be interested in connecting with their young adults.

You will need to get a commitment from each of the parishes to help financially and to support the program. Seek out the people who are interested. Before you approach them, try to list everything needed to make the program work, including the minister's salary with benefits, office space, office equipment, and supplies.

2. Once the parishes that will be participating are in place, gather representatives from each parish to **establish the vision.** The group will need to work together to accomplish the following:

a. Name what each parish hopes the areawide young adult ministry will accomplish, and in what time frame. Set some realistic, clear, quantifiable goals. These goals will need to be agreed upon by the young adult minister before he or she is hired. What will it take to call the ministry successful after two years? Given the size and nature of the parishes and neighborhoods, how many young adults will need to be connected the first year to call it a success? How big should the mailing list be after the first year? How many young adults should be connected in some leadership role? What type of activities would the group like to see offered? Prioritize that list. Are there any particular groups that should be formed (small faith groups, young married couples, grief support, etc.)? How often do the parish contact people want a progress report, and in what form (written report, phone conversation, lunch meeting, quarterly updates, yearly review)? How much of a commitment is each parish willing to make?

b. Discuss where the central office will be, and which parishes can open their doors to specific types of events. Young adults do not mind driving to get to where they want to be. The meetings and events will rotate among the participating parishes and other appropriate spaces. A procedure will need to be worked through to reserve meeting space at the various parishes.

c. Finances are usually the biggest issue, and responsibility should be divided however the participating parishes see fit. One parish will need to take responsibility for putting the young adult minister on its payroll. The other parishes then provide their share of that salary and other expenses. In addition to an office, the director of the regional young adult ministry will need a computer, a phone line, a computer line, access to a fax and copy machine, and a budget for printing, postage, supplies, and miscellaneous expenses. The salary should be comparable to the salaries of other professional ministers in the parish and diocese and based on their education, skills, and previous experience. As with the parish-based young adult ministry, every event should be designed to pay for itself.

d. Write a job description for the position of young adult minister. It might resemble that shown on the following page.

e. Create a search committee and a timeline for finding and hiring the most qualified individual, someone with a passion for this age group. He or she must be able to relate to the joys and struggles of young adults. This might not be someone who went right into ministry after graduation. Consider people who have been working "in the real world." They bring a perspective that ministers right out of school often lack. Look for someone with a dream of what can be. Finally, you have to find someone who is not afraid of a hard day's work.

f. Develop a plan for communications with the new young adult minister on a regular basis to discuss progress and provide support. This might be accomplished by appointing a staff member or two to sit on the advisory board that will be created.

3. Create an **advisory board.** This board can be made up of one or two staff people from each participating parish and several interested parents of young adults. If a parish is not willing or able to provide a supportive staff person with an interest in the success of young adult ministry, the ministry will not be successful. Excuses include "no one is available" and "there is too much going on right now." If there is not a staff member willing to work with you, young adult ministry is not yet a high priority in that parish. That is good information to have. Graciously thank the parish representatives, and ask if they would reconsider the following year. What you need are people who can attend a monthly brainstorming meeting. They are not there to do the planning, but rather to provide advice, support, and guidance in line with the vision and goals agreed upon earlier.

One regional young adult minister was asked what was most important in the success of her outreach. She responded, "Getting the finances and having the pastor's ear." We know how busy staff members are. That is why we are engaging in regional young adult ministry in the first place. If they do not see the importance of supporting the ministry, it cannot move forward with them. It is critically important to keep the advisory board together.

During the first year, the advisory board should try to meet once a month. It is a good way of supporting young adult ministers, keeping them

Director of Regional Young Adult Ministry Office

Position description: Six Catholic parishes in the western suburbs of the Archdiocese of Chicago are seeking a highly motivated, energetic individual to create, direct, and maintain a regional outreach to young adults: women and men in their twenties and thirties, married and single. This position requires a high degree of professionalism, a passion for this age group, and the ability to work well with parish staff members and volunteers.

Reporting: The Director of Young Adult Ministry will report to the pastors of each parish, with the assistance of an advisory board made up of parish staff members.

Specific responsibilities:

- establish contacts and relationships with staff and parish members
- use direct personal invitation to reach out to young adults in all parishes
- develop and maintain a master database of young adults in their twenties and thirties in all parishes
- listen and respond to the expressed needs of those young adults
- plan and execute monthly advisory board meetings
- invite young adult volunteers to assist in the mission of gathering their young adult peers and coordinate their efforts
- with volunteer support, plan and host social, serious, spiritual, and service events around relationship, faith, and work issues
- create newsletters, brochures, public service announcements, etc., as necessary to promote the events hosted through the ministry
- work with the advisory board to obtain additional funding when necessary
- document progress

Qualifications: Minimum bachelor's degree, strong written and verbal communication skills, exemplary organizational skills; flexible work hours a must; ministerial experience preferred.

accountable to the parishes, and making sure the ministry is headed in the right direction. The parish liaisons can also keep other staff members informed of progress and upcoming opportunities for young adults. Without a regular point of contact—with members of all parishes—young adult ministry becomes lost in the shuffle, and people begin to question whether or not good things are happening. This is especially true since not all parish staff members will see the young adult minister every day.

Letters, bulletin announcements, and other forms of publicity will not be able to accomplish what direct contact with an advisory board can. In addition to meeting with the advisory board, the young adult minister should plan to meet one-on-one with each pastor yearly. At the meeting with each pastor, a binder can be presented complete with a description of each event and group, brochures, photos, expense reports, a copy of the volunteer log, and a copy of the complete mailing list, which specifies how many of the young adults who participated were from each parish. (Preparing this binder is itself a good volunteer project for one of the young adult parishioners). Communication is essential, and accountability to your funding source will keep the funds flowing.

The advisory board also helps to set long-term goals. Where do you want to be in three years? In five years? In ten years? Is it time to add new parishes? Do you need to hire additional staff? Are there additional funding sources that should be approached? Is it time to apply for a grant to support a specific component of the ministry? How do you cover expenses when the ministry begins to expand and costs rise? The advisory board becomes an advocate for the program.

A final responsibility of the advisory board is to help the minister create a structure so solid that when he or she leaves, the ministry is left intact and can continue under new leadership.

4. Seek out and nurture **a group of young adult leaders** whose time and gifts will be valuable in developing the ministry and supporting particular events. These young adult volunteers should be invited from each of the participating parishes; the advisory board parish representatives might be able to suggest potential candidates. Unlike the role of advisory board, that of these volunteers is to assist with short-term goals and projects.

There are two ways of going about creating this level of support. Either can be successful. The first is to establish a group of core leaders who will work with the young adult minister for a specified amount of time (six months or a year). Under this model, leaders will get to know one another well, the group can build momentum, and the minister will know who can be counted on to accomplish particular tasks. Some leaders prefer the consistency that this model offers.

Another approach—and the one we prefer—is to recruit young adult volunteers as needed on a project-by-project basis. The minister's role is to personally invite people with particular gifts into a given project for the duration of that project. When the project is completed, they are graciously thanked and their commitment is ended. This approach fits well with the lifestyles of young adults. They come and go quickly. Most have "busy seasons" in their jobs, when it becomes more difficult to keep a commitment to the ministry. But with various projects happening at different times of the year, most can make themselves available for a project or two.

In this model, the young adult minister has the opportunity to work with a group of people for the duration of a project and then assess who worked well and who did not. Those who worked well will be invited into a leadership role in the future. Those who did not can be redirected into other ways to share their gifts in the future. It is not uncommon to invite some of the most talented volunteers to help on numerous projects, as their time allows. And you avoid the unpleasant task of having to "fire" a volunteer who, for whatever reason, did not move the project forward. Also, those who want to help but simply do not have the time year round do not need to feel guilty. Some of the best volunteers have their "pet project" and they give it their all—once a year. Each year they come back fresh and ready to improve on last year's success, after a nice long break. This approach also motivates the young adult minister to keep seeking out new talent, because it takes more people to get the work done.

5. Fill the following young adult **volunteer positions** as needed:

Parish liaison: communicate upcoming activities back to the parish through bulletin announcements, pulpit announcements, special mailings, etc.

Communications: assist with the newsletter and publicity for specific programs.

Administration: help in the office: data entry for mailing list, filing, phone calls, mailings, etc.

Computer support: program database, design and maintain web page, send monthly e-letter, etc.

Social coordinators: help to brainstorm, plan, and host social events.

Serious coordinators: help to brainstorm, plan, and host serious events.

Spiritual coordinators: help to brainstorm, plan, and host spiritual events.

Service coordinators: help to brainstorm, plan, and host service opportunities.

6. Following the strategies presented in the parish-based young adult ministry section, offer a wide **variety of opportunities** for young adults to gather. Give the outreach a name and a logo so that there is immediate recognition when publicity is presented in the parish bulletin, the local press, or through the mail. Evaluate every program, and host listening sessions where young adults can share their suggestions.

7. Arrange a meeting between the young adult minister and the coordinating board to **finalize the goals** for the first two years of the ministry. Those goals can be revised as time progresses, but they need to be in place, and both parties need to have agreed to them. It is the young adult minister's responsibility to present a strategy for reaching those goals.

8. Send to all sponsoring parishes a **quarterly** report of activities specifying the number of people who attended each activity. The funding sources need to know what they are getting for their money. The pastors are getting pressure from their finance people: Is this worth our money? They have to be able to explain why it is. Some years ago a regional outreach program was discontinued because those running it did not stay accountable to the parishes that were sponsoring them. Trust alone is not enough. Accountability is required. Quarterly, factual reports need to be written and distributed to all funding sources. People also want to know if young adults from their parishes are really participating. The list of participants should be distributed to them. Let them know that their people are being served. Include the logo, the list of volunteers, and the list of attendees for each event. When things are successful, we talk in quantity, "Everyone was there!" When things do not go well, we talk about quality: "But there was good sharing." Compile all the data for the annual

meeting with the pastors. After the second year, have a team of young adults compile a two-year report. People are willing to help when you can verbalize what you need. And it is not often that young adults are given the opportunity to show off their work to a group of pastors.

Consider everything the first year a pilot project. This is not a packaged program guaranteed to succeed. It is a well-thought-out experiment, with great potential to make a difference in many people's lives. The pastors and parishes are all taking a risk. If it works, everyone benefits. If it does not, the goals need to be revisited and revised.

Expect the second year to be a great deal stronger than the first. It is going to take time to connect with parish staffs and young adults. It is also going to take time to spread the word that good things are happening in the area. It is largely a process of building trust.

Don't be discouraged if any of the participating parishes choose to leave the program. Needs and priorities change. If that happens, meet with the staff members on the advisory board to find another parish to bring into the ministry. Moreover, not all parishes are able to be as supportive as they initially indicate they will be. Open communication is important. Do your best to keep them connected. Perhaps another staff member needs to be invited onto the advisory board. Or perhaps a member of the parish council is available. Do the best you can to finish out the year with them, and then together decide if it makes sense for them to continue in the program. Their support is as important as their financial contribution; do not settle for one without the other.

Finally, consider co-sponsoring events with the diocesan office. Our summer Theology-on-Tap program was hosted in one areawide outreach in three different parishes on three different evenings for four consecutive weeks. Young adults are mobile. They were given the opportunity to connect with a superb catechetical program on any of twelve evenings, so they could pick the night that worked best for them. The diocesan office mailed a newsletter to its mailing list of over twenty-seven thousand young adults. The regional director did some local publicity by mailing letters and flyers from her office. The parishes could also have put out letters and flyers for their particular nights. We are trying to give people many ways to experience the church. In this situation, we gave the church many ways to reach out to its people.

Chapter 9

Young Adult Ministry at the Diocesan Level

Occasionally we are asked why any diocese even needs a Young Adult Ministry Office. A diocesan Young Adult Ministry Office can play a vital role in the church today. While the local parish will always be the primary and, for many people, the only experience of the Catholic Church, a diocesan Young Adult Ministry Office can have three valuable functions:

1. It should be the best **resource** the diocese has for learning about and working more effectively with its young adult people.

2. It should be an **advocate** for young adults at parish and diocesan levels of church.

3. It should provide **pastoral ministry** directly to young adults by developing groups and programs throughout the diocese specifically for them.

Let's be honest. Many young adults will readily mention that there is very little activity in their parish that either appeals to them or specifically meets their needs. A diocesan office for young adult ministry can function as a type of parish focusing exclusively on the needs and experiences of young adults.

The Diocesan Office as Resource

As a resource, the Young Adult Ministry Office works directly with parishes and parish ministry personnel to develop their sensitivity and outreach toward young adults. The office should make parish personnel aware that it is not sufficient simply to establish a parish young adult group.

A parish young adult group will not always be the most effective approach to the relationship between young adults and their church. Sometimes it might, in fact, aggravate the problem that exists between many young adults and the church. It may be saying that to be a good Catholic means joining the young adult group. Many young adults, not just Catholics, are not joiners. Their human needs are not always properly met by joining a club, program, or community activity.

As a resource to the local parish, the Young Adult Ministry Office can suggest strategic ways to involve young adults in the life of the parish, to invite their presence, and to respond to their needs. Many young adults do not experience welcome when they approach the parish to celebrate their marriages, baptize their children, or even bury their parents. A Young Adult Ministry Office staff, knowledgeable about the young adult world, its needs, values, and experiences of church, can offer some suggestions for relationship and dialog at these critical young adult human moments of love, new life, and death.

The Young Adult Ministry Office can work with individual parishes and clusters of parishes to develop effective young adult groups. In every parish some people are more involved in the life of their community; they have time and a personal need to gather with people of like interest, age, and background. They have a need for a social or spiritual component in their lives, which can be met by gathering with others. In many parishes, people with these needs, or who think the parish can respond to these needs, are few. Therefore, it is often necessary to gather young adults from a number of parishes in order to develop a strong, healthy, and effective young adult group.

This office can be a leaven for other diocesan agencies. Many diocesan offices are lacking the presence of young adults in their work. A Young Adult Ministry Office can be a resource to change that. It can assist the Office for Separated and Divorced Catholics in reaching young adults who have already participated in the painful experiences of divorce or separation. It can work with the Office of Marriage and Family Life to develop support groups for the early years of marriage. It can assist the Chancery Office in explaining the annulment process and encouraging people to begin the process. The diocesan Office of Peace and Justice can benefit greatly from the life experience of many young adults. Some young adults can bring a wealth of pro-life experiences to the diocesan

Respect Life Office. Many teachers in Catholic schools are young adults; a diocesan Young Adult Ministry Office can be an excellent resource for assisting with the faith development of our teachers in Catholic schools.

Finally, a Young Adult Ministry Office should be a resource for the bishop of the diocese. Not only can the office assist the bishop in his understanding of the needs of young adults, but it can also provide him with opportunities to gather with them. The presence of the bishop can be seen as the "symbol" of the importance of these Catholic people and a ministry to them. The Young Adult Ministry Office can provide an annual opportunity for the bishop to preside at Mass with young adults in the cathedral. He can also be called upon to serve as teacher of the faith or as a pastoral presence at an event.

The staff of the Young Adult Ministry Office should be the "experts" about young adults, their place in the church, their needs, and their lifestyles. The office should be a resource on behalf of young adults to the rest of the church.

The Diocesan Office as Advocate

An advocate is needed for young adults in our church today. On all levels of church life, someone must ask the question, "Where are our young adults?" and assist in making their presence felt. A diocesan Young Adult Ministry Office fills this role.

Advocacy by the Young Adult Ministry Office extends to local parishes. It simply means that this agency is interested in seeing that parishes are sensitive to the presence (or lack of presence) of their young adults. The office might offer suggestions to local parish staffs to improve their integration of young adults into the life of the parish. Sometimes the office must simply ask the question, "Are the young adults in your parish present and active? Is there any help we might be able to offer you in your ministry to them?"

Advocacy might also involve contacting leaders in several parishes about the possibility of an areawide outreach to young adults (see chapter 8).

The Young Adult Ministry Office will also be an advocate for young adults and their concerns with other diocesan offices. For example, with the Office for Separated and Divorced Catholics it will help assure that

Young adults fill Holy Name Cathedral every summer for the Theology-on-Tap Mass, led by Cardinal Francis George.

ministry and support groups include younger Catholics. Young adults who have suffered the pain of separation and divorce might need a group of their own to deal with their particular life situations. Most Phoenix support groups are made up of people over the age of forty-five, and their issues are "family" issues. For many young adults that is not the separation or divorce experience. Usually no children are involved, and, if children are involved, they are very young.

A strong relationship should exist between the Young Adult Ministry Office and the diocesan Vocation Office. Young adult Catholics should be a major target group for vocation directors and recruiters. The Young Adult Ministry Office should support leadership retreats with the Vocation Office. Such retreats can bring together (by personal invitation) young adult leaders to explore their leadership role in the church. As natural leaders, they should be given the call to serve the world through the church as workers in our world, as ordained or professed religious leaders, as parish ministers or church lay ministers, or as full-time, part-time, or sometime volunteers.

This question was asked of a number of young adult ministers: "Have you been contacted by the Evangelization Office in your diocese about collaborating on outreaches to young adults?" The answer heard most often: "No." One of the primary targets of Catholic evangelization should be young adults. Single or married, they are the least present group in the church. The knowledge and wisdom gained about young adults by the Young Adult Ministry Office must be used by the Evangelization Office and any diocesan agency that ministers to Catholics in their twenties and thirties.

If there are other diocesan offices whose mission is to assist with various situations (divorce, newly married, grieving), but who are not reaching young adults and cannot do more, don't take no for an answer. Do it yourself. We may not do it as well as they would, because we are lacking the resources, but we'll soon have something to offer. Gather some folks. Get some things started. Later on check back with them.

Again, many Catholic school teachers are young adults. Wouldn't it make sense for Catholic school leaders to work with the Young Adult Ministry Office to design the ongoing religious formation of its young adult teachers? For many of those teachers there is no ongoing religious formation. We must remember that an entire segment of the Catholic young adult population received very little substantive catechetical training. Among them are many of today's Catholic school teachers, who now are the formal catechists of the Catholic tradition for the next generation. Are we developing a vicious circle? An effective Young Adult Ministry Office should be able to work with school officials to prepare an ongoing program for its teachers. Not only would it give them the catechetical skills to prepare second graders for their first holy communion. It would also share with those teachers—some for the first time since their own communion preparation days—the value of the Eucharist in their own adult lives and personal religious practice.

The Diocesan Office as Pastoral Ministry

The third function of a Young Adult Ministry Office is pastoral ministry. Diocesan young adult personnel are not managers of an office, but ministers to a people. They are the pastors to young adults in the diocese. The term "pastor" is not being used in a canonical sense or in a way that usurps the position, prominence, or importance of the parish pastor. Young adult ministry is a hands-on job; it is not a desk job. The young adult ministers will be the primary Catholic Church presence for a significant number of young adults. They will broker the relationship between young adults and the church. They are the bearers and the proclaimers of the faith to young adults who might not be able to find a niche in a parish at this time in their lives. They might find their place and the value of the faith through the pastoral ministry of the Young Adult Ministry Office, its staff, and its programs. In other words, the work of young adult ministry will be the "parish" for many young adults at this time in their lives.

This pastoral ministry has three forms: outreach, presence, and programs.

Outreach

Young adult ministry is one of the few Catholic outreaches to an age group of people (women and men, married and single, in their twenties and thirties) rather than to people in a particular state in life (single, married, divorced, widowed, parent). This presents a great opportunity to young adult ministers to reach out to all people who are young adults. "You work with singles?" "No, I work with young adults." "It's for college grads?" "No, for all young adults." "Your ministry must be to working professionals." "No, it's for anyone in their twenties and thirties."

The number of young adults who are reached by the church is the measure of a successful diocesan young adult ministry, not the number who attend events. The purpose is to present the tradition of the faith to young adults and offer them opportunities to experience that tradition, if and when they choose. Consequently, the first outreach strategy is simply to gather names of Catholic young adults from almost any source. Those people can be sent a personal letter, newsletter, or e-mail. The purpose is to let young adults know that in their diocese there is a place within the Catholic Church that cares for them, is truly interested in them, and is willing to do things with and for them.

In this form of pastoral ministry we can share articles about the Catholic faith and its importance in people's daily lives. We can update religious practices for the adult years. We can address the myriad of human life issues experienced by young adults. We can tap into the altruism of young adults by offering them places and opportunities to volunteer their time and talent. The ministry can be a forum for their own reflections on faith, parish life, and church experiences, and for their questions and shared stories about being Catholic. It can take the form of a question-and-answer series about things religious or about the place of religion and personal faith in their world. Written announcements, newsletters, and e-mail can present information about places where young adults gather for social activities, worship, serious conversation, and volunteering. This "printed" pastoral ministry is a type of church bulletin just for young adults. Let it be seen as a diocesan newspaper, though published only occasionally, for those who probably do not read or subscribe to the diocesan newspaper.

One diocesan director of young adult ministry was told rather cynically by his superior that he should be prepared to justify the expense of printing and mailing a newsletter to over three thousand young adults. The director responded by relating this comment by a woman in her late twenties: "I have been on your mailing list for years, but I have not attended anything you've sponsored. I'm at this program tonight because my father is dying, and I just need some help to figure things out." Pastoral ministry to a faceless name and address took flesh when the church was able to offer comfort and counsel at a significant human (and profoundly spiritual) moment in life.

All too often, parish life revolves around school-aged families and senior citizens. A Young Adult Ministry Office reaches out to people who do not fit comfortably into either of these categories.

Presence

Another form of pastoral ministry to young adults is presence: opportunities for young adults to be present to each other, and for the church to be present to them. We can never underestimate the value that young adults find in being with their peers. One of the most often expressed needs of young adults is to find people with whom to share their values and their time.

It is also very important for diocesan young adult ministers to be present to young adults. There is a great value in just "being" and not always "doing." Being present to young adults puts a very human face on the Catholic Church. Too many young adults have had little if any contact with Catholic Church personnel since their school days. A ministry of presence permits listening, compassionate caring, and support to people who are searching for the value of the church in their daily lives. Sometimes a simple presence can be more important than understanding church teaching at this time in life.

Programs

As we have seen there are four types of programs in which young adults can participate: social, serious, spiritual, and service (see p. 50).

Social Programs: The easiest way to gather people is socially: all you are asking for is their presence. Social situations are opportunities to meet people, have a good time, build relationships, and, for young adult ministers, discover those young adults who will be invited into positions of leadership.

Serious Programs: "Serious" programs include counseling and mentoring young adults, as well as support groups focusing on specific life experiences such as marriage, divorce, grieving, recovery, and various Twelve Step activities. Other serious programs include workshops, special sessions focusing on important young adult issues such as personal relationships and work, and young adult conference days.

Spiritual Programs: Spiritual programs include worship, prayer, retreats, and days of reflection, as well as spiritual direction, Scripture study, catechetical development, and small faith groups. Young Adult Sunday Masses, annual retreats, and programs on Scripture, theology, and faith in daily life are important for young adults who are searching for the value of the Catholic faith.

Service Programs: Volunteering is an intrinsic ingredient of any young adult ministry. It is a way for young adults to share their gifts and time in service to others. For many young adults, service has played an important role in their lives already; perhaps it began at the time of confirmation or through participation in a youth group or campus ministry program. Many young adults are looking for places to make a continued contribution with their time and talent, and often they do not know where to find service or volunteer opportunities. Many parishes have service opportunities in a ministry of care to the sick and shut-ins in the parish or are looking for volunteer catechists, athletic coaches, or youth group leaders. Frequently however, young adults are not that parochial. They are looking beyond the parish to the larger community for opportunities to serve the homeless, the poor, the sick, and those less fortunate in the world.

For other young adults, less affiliated with the church, a pastoral ministry that provides opportunities for service becomes a point of reentry. They will begin to see the value that faith can have in the world. Some young adults are restless with "just working for a living." Though it pays the bills and develops personal skills, it might not be very fulfilling. Some want to do more and be more. Invitations to serve and to enter into the human drama of other people's lives can complement a career or job and allow questions of meaning to be addressed.

A Full-Time Job

Diocesan young adult ministry is a lot of work. It is not so much an office to be staffed as a ministry to be accomplished. It is also fascinating and exciting church work. The approach is the opposite of what the church has done for people during their educational years. During those years of catechetical training, church ministers presented the faith to people who did not have the life experience to make it meaningful. Young adult ministry presents the faith to people who now have life coming at them faster than they can make sense of it. It is faith that helps us make sense of things. Young adult ministry done well can give today's young adults back the religious tradition that offers meaning and hope to their lives.

Because of what is happening in their lives during these years—the loves, the joys, the disappointments, the possibilities, the fears, and the hopes—young adults are beginning to look toward religion to help them be more fully alive. Some approach church with curiosity, others with hunger, others with a need to heal brokenness, others looking for a way to celebrate a rite of human passage, and still others looking for a home. Our challenge is to respond by showing them what good church is and does, by connecting them to others their age who share their values, and by providing opportunities that address their needs.

Effective diocesan young adult ministry is a full-time job. All too often in many dioceses it is a part-time position connected to another ministry. Part-time jobs yield partial results, especially since the other "part" of the part-time job frequently takes more time, energy, and money than the young adult ministry. Young adults deserve much more from their church than a partial response. If the nonpresence of so many young adult Catholics is admitted and understood, there should be little resistance to a full-time diocesan office.

Effective young adult ministry is not a hyphenated office, as in Youth-Young Adult Ministry or Campus-Young Adult Ministry. Effective young adult ministry does not resemble youth ministry and should not be confused with it. More than that, young adults are not *youth*. They react negatively when they are identified with youth, even if only by a title on a letterhead. And although many people affected by campus ministry are, in fact, young adults, the strategy and pastoral approach of campus ministry are very different from those of young adult ministry. Those who carry the hyphenated titles of "youth-young adult minister" or "campus-young adult minister" will attest to the fact that it often leads to confusion of roles and ministerial outreach, as well as less than the hoped for results. Very often there is a lack of sufficient time to do justice to either.

Ministry to young adults should be a diocesan priority. Every office, agency, and parish should examine the impact of its work on young adult Catholics. And if few young adults are the recipients of parish or agency ministry, then business as usual is not effective. The longer young adults live disconnected from the church, the less reason they have to participate. Certainly, marriages and baptisms will be celebrated; their children will receive first holy communion and attend some catechism classes. After all, they need something to live by. But on a day-to-day, week-to-week, year-in-year-out basis, more Catholics will be so in name and not in practice.

Paying for Young Adult Ministry

The church finance issue involved in young adult ministry was put in this context by a bishop: "This ministry to young adults is really a form of evangelization. After all, if they are not a part of the church, who will be around in ten years to pay the bills?" The bishop was right and wrong. It is evangelization. If they are not around, fewer people will be paying the bills for every aspect of church ministry. He was wrong in his dating of the problem. The lack of younger people active, present, and paying in the church *today*, not ten years from now, is one of the major components of the financial crisis in almost every diocese. There are fewer people present in parishes who are being asked to pay more of the bills. Fewer and *older* Catholics are being asked to give more of their resources to alleviate the financial problems of parishes and dioceses.

Only a few years ago, by the age of twenty-five people were registered

in a parish, their children were attending, or about to attend, the parish
school, they had established roots in their neighborhood, and they were
contributing to the support of their parish and school. Today, many young
adults, and their money, are not as present. In other words, an effective
young adult ministry is good fiscal policy, for it will provide people *now*
to help pay the bills. "How do you pay for young adult ministry?" Perhaps
the answer is clearer now: *Young adults can pay for young adult ministry.*

Young adults are part of the consumer society. They pay for what they
get; they buy what they like. Provide them with a sense of belonging.
Take them seriously. Make room for them on Sunday and throughout the
week. Welcome them to church programs. Treat them lovingly at their
moments of return. Make them recipients of gracious hospitality. If all
this is accomplished, the call to Christian stewardship will be heard.

Young Adult Ministry on a Diocesan Level: The Chicago Experience

Just as diocesan young adult personnel function much like pastors, if a
diocesan Young Adult Ministry Office works well, it will function as a type
of young adult parish. Like a parish, a diocesan office can provide prayerful
worship, gatherings to enhance spiritual growth, religious education, and
opportunities for service. It is a parish for an age group, not a geographical
area. A young adult office can invite into greater participation many young
adults who do not express parish affiliation. Young adults in general do
not register for many things, including Catholic parishes. The people least
likely to register to vote are those in their early twenties.

As a frame of reference, we will take a look at the specifics of the
Young Adult Ministry Office for the Archdiocese of Chicago. We are one
of many diocesan agencies that fall under the umbrella of the Department
of Evangelization and Catechesis. As a diocesan office, we attempt to
connect with young adults in four ways:

1. We provide an outreach to young adults who may not be associated
   with any parish.

2. We provide experiences of Catholicism, acting as parish in many
   ways. We offer worship, community building, preparation and admin-

istration of the sacraments, religious education, and a social justice component.

3. We organize large-scale events that are beyond what an individual parish is usually able to do.

4. We assist parishes in working with their own young adults.

Here is our mission statement:

Young Adult Ministry is the outreach service of the Catholic community in the Archdiocese of Chicago to young adults, women and men in their twenties and thirties, married and single. Young Adult Ministry has a very simple purpose: to put people in contact with each other and to offer some alternatives and supplements that may not be experienced in our culture. We try to respond to questions like these:

> *Are there people around who share my values?*
>
> *The bars are good, but is there anything else?*
>
> *How do you meet good people once you've moved here?*
>
> *What does it mean to be a person of faith today?*
>
> *Is there any decent worship around?*
>
> *Where can I give some of my time and talent?*

The questions in the mission statement are questions young adults ask. They come out of their vocabulary and the hungers of their lives, and we have built young adult ministry around them. Here we will explore those questions a bit more deeply.

1. *Are there people around who share my values?* Young adults are looking for people who are like them and who have had similar experiences. Young adults see the value of community and strive to be connected.

2. *The bars are good, but is there anything else?* Bars are the cultural oases for young adults to meet people. As good as they are in providing a meeting place, many young adults are looking for something more.

3. *How do you meet good people once you've moved here?* Young adults are the most mobile part of the U.S. population. Some of their movements are obvious: from school back home, from their family home to their own home, and from their hometown to a new town. Some

young adults relocate within the same geographic area. Moving is based on job opportunities, financial situations, and relationships. Wherever their movement takes them, they are seeking people with whom they can share life, become friends, and do things together. Simply changing an address can create loneliness in some young adults.

4. *What does it mean to be a person of faith today?* This is becoming an increasingly more important issue as we hear about the spiritual hunger of young Americans. People tell us they do not know what it means to be Catholic—even those who have gone to church every Sunday all their lives. They are spiritually restless, with a hunger they do not know how to fill. Without using any church language, they ask how to grow deeper in their relationship to God.

5. *Is there any decent worship around?* Some young adults have had very positive worship experiences in parishes they have previously attended or youth and campus ministry programs in which they have participated. They know what good church is. Now they are looking for similar worship experiences as young adults. Others are just "turned off" by what they perceive to be dull Masses lacking inspiration, life, and people their age.

6. *Where can I give some of my time and talent?* This is a generation of people who think about giving back. Many are highly altruistic. They are concerned with building a better world. For them, young adult ministry is a resource to do that.

In 1977 when the Young Adult Ministry Office began under the direction of Fr. John Cusick, a budget was allotted for his part-time position. Now, the office has grown to include three full-time paid positions: two pastoral ministers and an office assistant. Additionally, the office uses the support of over a thousand volunteers annually. The time they share and the talent they give is essential to the continued growth and effectiveness of the office.

Often we are asked for the job descriptions of the staff members in our office. On the two pages that follow we present those job descriptions as they have evolved over the years.

Archdiocesan Young Adult Ministry Office: Director

Creates, directs, and maintains the ministry to young adults, women and men, married and single, in their twenties and thirties, within the Archdiocese of Chicago. Specific responsibilities include:

- Create programs and other forms of outreach to young adults in the archdiocese.

- Work with parish staffs, deans, and vicars to create and develop a ministry to, for, and with young adults in parishes, clusters, and vicariates.

- Work with the Young Adult Ministry Office staff as necessary.

- Train office staff in the philosophy and theology of Young Adult Ministry, Chicago-Style.

- Train young adult leaders on a parish level.

- Work with and train volunteers for projects and programs on an archdiocesan level.

- Prepare, present, and live within the budget for Young Adult Ministry.

- Work with various archdiocesan agencies (Vocations, Evangelization, Ministry in Higher Education, Family Ministry, Office for Catechesis, etc.) in mutual areas of interest.

- Attend and contribute to various archdiocesan meetings.

- Manage an office staff and work responsibilities.

- Counsel young adults on a one-time and ongoing basis.

- Celebrate young adult Masses and participate in various sacramental moments (marriages, baptisms, reconciliation, etc.).

- Preach at least one of the two annual young adult retreats.

- Attend national young adult meetings.

- Accept invitations to speak at gatherings about young adult issues throughout the U.S.

- Deal with innumerable phone calls and requests for every conceivable and inconceivable service for young adults.

- Brainstorm and try new ideas yearly.

Archdiocesan Young Adult Ministry Office: Associate Director

In conjunction with the director of Young Adult Ministry, administers, co-ordinates, maintains, and develops the ministry to young adults. Specific responsibilities include:

- Organize, execute, and follow up archdiocesan young adult programs.

- Invite, work with, and manage volunteer committees for programs and activities.

- Manage and maintain computers, select and upgrade software, and program when necessary.

- Provide leadership training of young adult leaders on a diocesan and parish level.

- Write, edit, and publish the quarterly newsletter, *Young Adult Ministry, Chicago-Style.*

- Maintain the Young Adult Ministry Office, its files, leader and parish lists, routine correspondence, staff meetings, telephone inquiries, and the vast number of nonprogrammed things that happen daily.

- Preach at various young adult events.

- Speak on young adult issues at various events within and beyond the archdiocese.

- Work with parish staff members and volunteers to provide quality opportunities for young adults on the parish level.

- Attend and contribute to archdiocesan meetings upon request.

- Respond to individual young adult needs and requests received in the mail, by e-mail, by telephone, and in person.

- Offer spiritual direction (short-term) upon request.

- Maintain records of young adult events, including statistical data, financial summaries, program evaluation, and strategies for improvement.

- Implement as many of the creative ideas as possible throughout the year.

Because the office functions largely as a parish for young adults, the Young Adult Ministry Office staff ideally includes a priest. The need for a priest at the sacramental moments of marriage, baptism, reconciliation, and, less frequently, illness and death, is great. If having a priest on the staff is not possible, the director will need to collaborate with priests who understand and work well with this age group and who can assist with sacramental moments, including young adult Masses.

The *office assistant* provides office support and assists, as needed, in maintaining and coordinating volunteers to help complete general office and committee work.

We have also created a *volunteer coordinator* position, which is itself a volunteer position. The role requires a commitment of two hours a week, but more time is needed prior to the publication of a newsletter and the two events the coordinator hosts. The volunteer coordinator makes connections between young adults interested in volunteering and social service agencies with volunteer needs. The responsibilities of the volunteer coordinator and more information about our Volunteers-in-Action program can be found in chapter 12.

Diocesan-Level Strategies

In designing and maintaining a diocesan outreach to young adults, many of the same principles used at the parish level are applicable. The Jesus Method of Organizing and finding ways to do the ordinary differently are appropriate here. Here are some additional suggestions for an effective diocesan outreach to young adults:

Create a Database

It is critical to keep a current list of all the young adults with whom you need to stay in contact.*

A well-crafted database not only will give you the essential information (name, address, phone, e-mail), but also can be used to create a profile for each young adult. Each database entry might include date of birth, hobbies, talents, skills, personal interests, events attended, financial

---

*The database for the Young Adult Ministry Office for the Archdiocese of Chicago was designed by David Barsotti. He donated his time and talent as a programmer. David used Microsoft Access to create the design. Further details about our database can be found in Appendix C.

Maintaining the database

The upkeep of the database is a good volunteer project. We have a group of people who each give us two hours a week when needed. For example, after our summer Theology-on-Tap program, over sixty parishes send us their list of participants. Volunteers assist with the timely entry of data for those participants. The Theology-on-Tap participants can then be contacted quickly, kept informed, and invited to attend future young adult events.

---

donations, volunteer support, leadership roles, and special needs. It has been our policy that all information on our Young Adult Ministry Office database is strictly confidential. Computer password protection can insure that confidentiality.

In our database we also keep track of languages spoken and musical talent. For both Theology-on-Tap, our summer program, and the FOCUS conference every spring, we assemble a young adult choir, complete with forty to fifty voices and ten to fifteen instrumentalists. Everyone who is coded on the database as a musician is invited to make great music with us. We also consult that list for retreats and other events with a musical component.

Gather names of young adults. At every young adult event, we ask people to complete a registration card. Those names and addresses are then checked against our mailing list. Those who are already on our list are coded for attendance at that event, and we confirm that we have their correct address, phone numbers, and e-mail address. If they are not on our list, they are added and then coded.

Ask parents of young adults. Many parents will gladly share the names and addresses of their young adult children. When Catholic parents are asked what the church can do for them, the most immediate and frequent response is, "Do something for my kids." Many of those "kids" are young adults. Place a bulletin notice that reads:

Attention parents of people in their twenties and thirties. We are hosting events that might be of interest to your young adult sons and daughters, and we want to contact them. Please send their names and addresses to . . .

> ### *What do you prefer for lunch?*
>
> Data on our conference registration form is now part of our regular database. It allows us to keep track of who is registered for what parts of the day, choices of workshops, all finances, meal choices, etc. We can look back to see what type of talks participants have attended, whether or not they have registered children for our day care, in what way they volunteered at the conference, if they have ever added an extra donation, even what they prefer for lunch.

Use the database. We can communicate with a target group according to the events they have attended. This helps immensely when deciding who should receive a mailing for upcoming programs. For example, if we have a speaker on the topic of spirituality, in addition to the general publicity we might send a letter of invitation to all who attended a retreat in the past year and those who attended the women's or men's day on spirituality.

Keep the database current. Young adults move frequently. Therefore it is essential to keep updating the list. Each mailing to the entire list should include "address service requested" below the return address. This can be costly, but it is more cost effective to receive address corrections and keep your list current than to keep mailing information out to people who will never receive it.

Offer assistance to parishes. Upon request, we can provide parishes with the names and addresses of anyone on our mailing list who either lives in a particular zip code or has attended an event in a particular area. That list of young adults can be printed to mailing labels and sent directly to the local parish. In this way we are able to help parishes find the young adults who have connected with us, but might not be registered at the parish. This is a good example of the diocesan office and the parish working together.

Write Letters

We believe in the "theology of the short note." In this age of electronic communication through faxes, e-mail, and form letters, a short, personal note of thanks can have a great impact on a young adult. It is becoming a totally unexpected but deeply appreciated form of communication. We also believe that it is an essential aspect of hospitality. The short note works well as a way to thank young adults we have met at a young adult event and let them know how much we appreciated their presence. The note might include an invitation to participate in another young adult event.

Produce a Quarterly Newsletter

We send out a newsletter four times a year to all twenty-seven thousand young adults on our mailing list. It is our most basic form of communication with our entire constituency, our quarterly opportunity to let them know that their Catholic Church has an interest in them. Our newsletter provides articles of interest, opportunities for volunteering, and details about upcoming programs. The articles focus on being people of faith and finding God in our everyday lives. Once a year the newsletter lists those parishes and organizations that offer quality opportunities for young adults. Providing those lists helps to maintain a good working relationship with parishes and organizations and helps us to be a better resource when people call looking for something in their neighborhood. Twice a year the newsletter includes our Volunteers-in-Action list, along with contact names and numbers so interested people can connect with an organization in need of their time.

Each issue of our young adult ministry newsletter contains a name and address form titled: "Share the Word." Young adults and other readers of our newsletter use this form to submit the names of friends, family, co-workers, and others who might benefit from being on the young adult ministry mailing list.

Our ministry is to all young adults within our archdiocese, including a large number of people we have never met and may never get to know. Through our quarterly newsletter, we extend to them the presence of the Catholic Church, which cares about them as young adults and invites them to participate more fully in Catholic life. We are there for them, and that is what matters most.

A good young adult ministry newsletter is made better by the talents and skills of young adult volunteers. Volunteers can suggest, write, and type articles, edit, add art work, take pictures and write captions, assist with layout, and proof the final copy. Local parish group leaders will also be happy to write about what good things are happening at their parishes for the extra exposure. However, the content and style of the young adult ministry newsletter should conform to the vision and mission of the Young Adult Ministry Office.

Our newsletters are produced and mailed every four months according to this plan:

September—Fall Issue	January—Winter Issue
Articles	Articles
Fall programs	Winter programs (give people something to do in the dead of winter)
Local parish opportunities	
Holiday happenings	Upcoming events
Volunteer opportunities	Share the Word section
Upcoming events	
Share the Word section	
March—Spring Issue	**June—Summer Issue**
The spring program—our annual FOCUS conference	Complete details on the Theology-on-Tap speaker/discussion series happening in more than sixty parishes simultaneously
Other upcoming events	
Share the Word section	Other upcoming events
	Share the Word section

Get On-line

A Young Adult Ministry Office website is essential. Since so many young adults work in the world of Internet technology, some may be willing and able to offer valuable assistance in making the website a useful tool in the diocesan outreach to young adults. Many young adults have Internet access at work, at home, or both, so an effective website can be as valuable as a printed newsletter. All the material in a printed newsletter should also be found on the Young Adult Ministry Office website.

It is also essential for an office to use e-mail in its electronic outreach to young adults. Consider a monthly e-letter. Whereas a printed newsletter might take weeks to write, edit, print, and mail, an e-letter can move from the writing to the mailing in a matter of minutes. An e-letter can highlight

Daily reflections

Once we got our web page up and running, we looked for ways to keep young adults visiting it on a regular basis. For example, in Lent of 2000, we posted a daily reflection and a suggested format for praying. Those reflections, based on the readings of the day, can be found in Appendix B. To take the idea a step further, ask young adults to join you in writing the reflections.

one particular activity or a series of events for young adults. Dioceses with a large e-mail list of young adults might wish to use a list hosting service, which will maintain an accurate e-mail address list. Such a service can be arranged at minimal cost or even free of charge. A Young Adult Ministry Office website can link young adults technologically to the entire Catholic world.

Since many parishes have their own websites, you might request that each parish have a link to the Young Adult Ministry Office website. In turn, the young adult office can have links to all the parishes that host young adult events.

Promote the Presence of the Bishop

The bishop can have three vital roles in the diocesan ministry to young adults: teacher, preacher, and person. Not only is the bishop the pastor of the diocese; he is also the chief teacher of the faith. When the diocesan Office of Young Adult Ministry sponsors a faith formation program, it should invite the bishop to be one of the speakers.

Annually the diocesan office should sponsor a Mass for all young adults, with the bishop as presider. This is a superb opportunity, not only to lead young adults in prayer, but also to preach the message of Jesus Christ to this spiritually hungry generation of Catholics. We are very fortunate in the Archdiocese of Chicago that our cardinal archbishop has spoken at our summer Theology-on-Tap program and presides annually at a Mass in our cathedral, attended by young adults who have participated in Theology-on-Tap.

There is a third "role" that our cardinal archbishop plays in the lives of the young adults of his archdiocese. He is also a person, and not just a functionary. He hosts a picnic on the lawn of his residence once a year for young adults. It is very important that the bishop be seen by young adults as personable—one who can socialize with young adults and enjoy their company.

Chapter 10

Principles for a Diocesan Ministry to Young Adults

Good ministry does not just happen; it is planned. This is certainly true for a diocesan ministry to young adults, which reaches out to a wide range of young adult people, their varied lifestyles, and their many backgrounds, talents, and skills. A diocesan ministry also faces the challenges presented by many dioceses and geographical areas blessed with people from various cultural and ethnic traditions. Here we offer ten principles for a diocesan outreach to young adults. Some of these ideas we have seen before in our discussion of local and regional ministries, but we mention them briefly again here because of their importance on the diocesan level as well. Likewise, many of the principles, guidelines, and strategies effective on the diocesan level are easily adapted to the local parish and regional levels.

Ten Principles

1. Put people before programs.

This sounds like an obvious strategy, but very often the opposite takes place. Time and effort are given to planning an initial young adult event without first answering the question, "Who do we want to be there?" Decide who are your key young adults. In other words, who are the ten to twenty young adults around whom you can build your ministry and whose presence will be the energy to make a young adult program successful? Then decide what you will do. If you begin with the right people, the likelihood of a successful event will be greater.

2. Put compassion before legalism.

Especially when young adults come asking for sacraments, be compassionate. Do not throw rules and laws at young adults without understanding where they are coming from and what they need. Avoid making unnecessary rules. You are the first one who is going to have to follow those rules, and you will be the first one to break them. A rule-driven sense of pastoral ministry is not pastoral at all. Try to lobby for young adults, knowing that there are times when some of them will not fit the parish norms. Let all sacramental preparation be moments of teaching and healing. Legalism will drive people further toward the edge of the church; compassion may bring them back closer to the altar.

This is compassion *before* legalism, not compassion *or* legalism. A compassionate ministerial style or a compassionate first gathering with young adults will permit a greater understanding on their part of the rules and laws that need to be part of any sacrament or group experience within the church.

3. Emphasize the adult, not the young.

All too often young adult ministry is confused with youth ministry. They are very different. Young adult ministry is directed toward adults. The language and the activities should be for adults. Gear it to people in their twenties and thirties, who put in long, hard work weeks and have other obligations. Do not treat them as children or, worse yet, teenagers. Listen to them, and respond to their adult needs.

4. Presume little; explain lots.

When it comes to the Catholic Church and to spiritual or religious matters, many young adults are in a learning mode. They have a hunger to know more about their faith, their church, and the customs and practices that make up our religious rituals. We have a church language young adults do not know. Almost everything about religion needs to be graciously explained to them. At Mass we stand, sit, kneel, and genuflect; they want to know why. On one Wednesday a year, our foreheads are marked with ashes in the form of a cross; though many young adults participate in that ritual, many do not know why. As young parents or godparents, they watch a child be anointed with oil. What's that all about? Caskets are surrounded by burning incense at the end of a Catholic funeral service. Rarely are they told why. Their hunger to know is real, and it seems that the list of things to be explained is limitless! Presume little; explain lots.

Exploring the Catholic culture

We host various sessions to help young adults understand particular aspects of their Catholic faith. Two of these are a church tour and an explanation of the Catholic Mass. We are a people of ritual and symbol. Both need to be explained. Our church tour meets in a Catholic church and is a visual opportunity to point to, look at, and explain the many symbols found in every Catholic church. It is also an opportunity for young adults to ask about things they have seen in churches and have always wanted to know what they meant. A church tour is a chance to explain holy water, a baptismal font, the sanctuary and sanctuary lamp, the tabernacle, the altar, the ambo, the Paschal candle, statues, religious art, candles, and devotional images.

We also present a session called "A Celebration of Catholic Mass and an Explanation." As a priest presides at an actual Mass, another person explains the meaning behind the many rituals that take place during every Mass.

Other presentations have been developed around special times of the year. One is called "An Adult Appreciation of the Christmas Story." Similar presentations can be done in the Lenten season, especially during Holy Week. Other sessions can take social celebrations and explore their Catholic roots, for example, Valentine's Day and Halloween. The Catholic culture has given the popular culture many celebrations.

5. *Avoid the use of church jargon.*

The term "evangelization" is used a lot among church professionals. It is not meaningful to young adults. Find another word. Avoid the phrase "Vatican II." That ecumenical council ended in 1965, before most of them were born, and its meaning can be ancient history to many of them. Avoid the word "community." Rather than being talked about, community should be experienced. If you use the word, be sure you can deliver the experience. We know what we mean by "family," but the culture defines family as mom, dad, and the kids. If you are not married with children, you know you do not belong. Define every religious term that you use. Religious words are just not in their vocabulary. If you need to use church language, be prepared to define your terms immediately upon using them. Keep in mind the adage: knowledge is power. When you help young adults understand their church, its rituals, and its vocabulary, you are empowering them to enter more fully into the life of their church and its practices.

6. Preach the God of our everyday lives.

God is found in the routine, in the ordinary. God has gotten to us before we ever thought of going to God. Our lives are sacred; God dwells with us, and everything around us can reveal God's presence. Let young adults know that their work is their vocation, that the work of their lives is making a difference and helping to build a better world. People love to be inspired. Let them know that their lives are important. God is with them. All gatherings with young adults can be moments of preaching and inspiring. Whether you have the microphone for two minutes or forty minutes, never miss the opportunity to remind people of who we are, how important we are in God's eyes, and what we are about in God's name. Remind young adults that they are called to be great and glorious people.

7. Recruit volunteers.

Most of what we do is possible only with volunteer help. Many highly skilled young adults loyally will share their time and talent. Hand pick your leaders, and personally invite them into the vision of what young adult ministry can be. But realize that if we make unreasonable demands on them, they will leave and not return. Make certain that there is never any guilt. Volunteers who do not fulfill their commitments will feel enough guilt on their own if you have established a good working relationship with them. Let them know that whatever time and energy they can share is greatly appreciated.

We keep a profile of our office volunteers, which includes their gifts and skills, as well as when they are available to volunteer and which projects they enjoy most. Detailed information about the effective use of volunteers can be found in chapter 12.

8. Build a positive reputation.

Church ministers usually define their work by the programs and activities they develop and direct. Interestingly, young adults evaluate much in their lives by reputation. Therefore, building a positive image and reputation of young adult ministry should equal the effort put forth in designing young adult programs and activities. The best way to build and maintain a positive reputation is to be conscious of the people involved. Work for a good balance of men and women, both on planning teams and in attendance at every activity. More people will consider attending if you have the reputation of being a place where young adults can mix and mingle. Do not hesitate to seek out the very popular young adults. Their presence and feedback can help shape the desired positive reputation.

9. Nurture young adult leaders.

Diocesan young adult ministry affords you opportunities to meet many more young adults than you would ministering in one parish. Keep a list of ten to twenty of the most interesting young adults you have met. They can be your leaders. Invite them for an evening of conversation. Discuss who they are and the talents they have been given. Then invite them to work with you for the good of the whole diocese.

It is important to connect leaders of young adult groups within your diocese. Invite them to a "Leaders Get-together" that you host. This gathering would encourage group leaders to act as resources for one another, share ideas, and promote their activities. In the Archdiocese of Chicago, the group leaders created an annual volleyball tournament, a good way for members of various groups to meet one another and connect socially.

10. Intervene when necessary.

There will be times when personality conflicts, differences of opinion, and bizarre behavior will occur. It is inevitable in any group. Sometimes there will be need for direct, personal intervention by the leadership. These situations cannot be willed away, nor can leadership pretend they are not important. If conflict is not resolved or destructive behaviors challenged, they can eat away at the very heart of a young adult ministry. It might become necessary, in as personal and caring a way as possible, for a leader to suggest that a person seek professional help or guidance. At other times, a leader might need to make a simple suggestion for someone to talk less and listen more. And, sadly, there may be times when, for the good of the ministry, the protection of certain people, or the future of young adult activities, a person must be asked no longer to attend. This is the most difficult part of any ministry position. However, if such situations are not dealt with quickly, caringly, and professionally, they can destroy young adult ministry.

Guidelines for Event Planning

It is not enough simply to decide on an event, create publicity, find a location, chill the beverages, fill the bowls with snacks, turn on the lights, set up the chairs, and open the door. As important as each of these can be, we also suggest the following guidelines:

1. Timing is everything.

Every young adult event must be planned around young adults' lifestyles and schedules. This seems so obvious, but often it does not happen this way. Often young adult events are planned around church schedules. For example, we plan no programs during certain sports seasons. If a particular team is in the baseball playoffs or the basketball finals, it makes no sense to host a young adult activity in competition. However, a young adult activity can be designed to include that sporting event, such as gathering to watch that event together on a big screen TV.

We rarely plan an event for Saturday mornings. After a long work week, Saturday morning is the time for young adults to run errands, do their laundry, or catch up on needed sleep or relaxation. Our Saturday winter programs begin at 1:00 p.m., and conclude by 6:00 p.m. We do not run into the evening because people go out on Saturday evenings. A much better time for young adults is Sunday night. It might not be a good time for the staff, because we have already worked part of the day and we are tired. But they are open to attending an event before the workweek begins again. Many young adults attend Mass on Sunday evenings. Some parishes host successful young adult gatherings immediately following their Sunday evening Mass.

We avoid hosting events during the first part of the summer. This is a busy social time when young adults are keenly interested in connecting with the many outdoor and summer opportunities for which they have been waiting for many months. We have discovered that the second half of the summer is a better time to schedule young adult activities. Now

> ### *Reaching out*
>
> We recently asked 150 young adults we know to give us the names and ad-
> dresses of a person or two who they know are Catholic, but who no longer
> come to church. The response was extremely positive. We personally con-
> tacted each person, by phone and by mail, and invited them all to our
> conference as our guests; the registration fee was waived. We were able
> to connect with a new group of people who might otherwise never have
> participated.

that they have settled into their summer schedules, they are often seeking
new and different activities. We have been very successful in hosting our
summer speaker and discussion series, Theology-on-Tap, from the week
after the Fourth of July through early August.

2. Much of young adult ministry is a pilot project.

That simply means it is experimental. Leaders are seeking new and creative ways to invite young adults into fuller participation in their church.
Since the ministry is new and experimental, mistakes will be made and
some things will fail. Don't be afraid of that. Too many great ideas never
find expression because the fear of failure prevents them from ever being
tried. We do not worry about having everything in place before creating
anything. If you are trying something just to see if it will work, you do not
even need everyone's approval. Go ahead and get it started. If it works,
great! Others will climb on board. If it doesn't work, pull it apart and
learn what to do differently next time. People are embarrassed or upset
by failure. That doesn't help. Even in our spiritual lives, we need to get
beyond failure to be free to take risks.

Too many great ideas are shut down by negative attitudes and worrying
about all that might go wrong. Another major stumbling block is waiting
for every detail to be taken care of before launching a program. We don't
have the luxury of that much time. Make it a pilot project, and keep
track of your results. Our programs are not always planned to the "nth
degree." We try things, get feedback, and make them better. We try, then
fix it, then try it again. You will serve more people, gain more wisdom,

and improve your skills quicker than if you wait for the ultimate event to be put in motion. In other words, don't just talk about it . . . do it!

3. Co-sponsor events with parishes.

We plan events and speaker series and invite parishes to co-sponsor them with us. We usually invite two types of parishes to co-sponsor events. The first are those parishes that already work well with their young adults. The second are those parishes that, after being coached in strategies and skills, can use this young adult event as a means of outreach to their young adults and creating a more effective ministry to them. Not only can we work together to design the co-sponsored program, but we can also help them to develop more opportunities for young adults to become active in their parish.

4. Begin with activities easy to plan and easy to execute successfully.

Everyone likes a winner; everyone enjoys success. Decide on the simplest young adult activity, and just do it. Those invited will be pleased, and there will be other positive results as well. The first is your own sense of accomplishment. The second is that the successful event can be referred to in future publicity for young adult activities. Hosting a successful first event will create some momentum and give you the strength to forge ahead.

5. Never run the same program the same way.

Habits can be deadly. When young adult activity is successful, there is often the temptation to repeat the event exactly the same way the next time. We may host a second event that is similar, but we should not do so without first evaluating what we liked and did not like about the first and listening to the feedback of the participants. Additionally, we always put new spins on the events we host. Ask, "How do you do the ordinary differently?" for each event. Be creative, and keep it fun. Sometimes we host the same program with minor revisions, but for an entirely different group of people or in a new location. Our annual list of young adult activities sponsored by the Young Adult Ministry Office is made up of two groups: successful events with a new twist and new events. It would get dull for us and for those we serve to do the same things the same way year after year. The mobility of young adults affects not only their addresses; it also influences their needs and wants. They are looking for new ways to participate in routine experiences.

6. Dream time is productive work time.

Once a year, set a full day aside to do some dreaming. Possible agenda items:

    a. Review the past year and list the strengths and successes

    b. List areas in which you hope to improve

    c. List three goals for each of the next three years

    d. Create an action plan for your primary goal for the next year

    e. Brainstorm possible new activities: What would you simply love to do? With whom would you like to make it happen?

Too many events hosted by our church are on autopilot. Year after year we host the same events the same way because we are expected to host them. Don't let that happen. Keep everything you offer fresh and energizing for you and the young adults you gather.

7. Effective young adult ministry is about marketing and sales.

We are in the "God business." Our task is to market the presence of God in the routine of daily life. We are selling to young adults the reality that their lives are sacred and the activity of God is found within the events of daily life. That seems to have been the marketing plan of Jesus. Jesus went from town to town, proclaiming the reign of God, and the crowds followed. That is our ministry too, and, like Jesus, we have to find good ways to do it. Be mission driven; do not wait for people to come to you. Most young adults simply won't. Be out there, selling and inviting.

8. The answer is not always a group.

Young adults approach us asking many questions and exhibiting various needs. The answer isn't always "Join this young adult group." In church work, we tend to compartmentalize, grouping like people together. Many young adults, however, will not participate in groups. They want good Sunday worship. They want to connect with their church. They want to share their gifts, contribute their time and talent, and help others. And they want to come into closer contact with their God. None of that requires that they "join" anything. Diocesan young adult ministry does not begin and end with creating young adult groups. It is necessary to create other opportunities and activities as well.

Provide young adults with opportunities to volunteer and to be more fully involved in worship. Create activities in which young adults can participate according to their concerns, needs, and interests. For example, plan a day that focuses on relationships for both single and married young adults. Those for whom relationships are an issue can attend this one-day activity. It is not necessary to be a group member, but simply a young adult with this interest. Though a parish young adult group can be very important, most young adults are "nonjoiners." By gathering young adults for occasional activities, there is a good chance that a greater number of people will be reached.

9. Never let money get in the way of a great idea.

How often have great ideas been killed when someone says, "We can't afford to do that"? Talk about the idea and what it might look like. If it seems exciting and possible, try to find a way to make it work. It is amazing how talented and resourceful you can become when you try to carry out a great idea. It is even possible to create some interesting financial plans to make a good idea happen. As important as money is to ministry, lack of funds should never kill a new idea.

10. Turn every young adult program into a happening.

Make every young adult event something exciting. Music, hospitality, refreshments, and décor can make all the difference. Very often young adults who do not know one another or do not know what to expect will come into an event quietly and separately. Have several people work the crowd, welcoming people as they arrive and introducing them to one another. Festive background music can create a comfortable atmosphere. Invite people to snack on munchies and enjoy a beverage of their choice. One of the principles of young adult ministry is to do the ordinary differently. Make it so exciting that people will want to return for more.

11. Get connected. There is no need to work alone.

You will never have the staff needed to do the job. That does not mean you are working alone. Hand pick leaders to assist you with events to help

Looking good

Our newsletter, *Young Adult Ministry Chicago-Style,* is put together for an adult audience. It has a sense of invitation to it, a sense of welcome. Use your best strategies, and the talents of young adults who are skilled at marketing and sales, to make your work look good. Do not be afraid to use the best techniques of the secular world to sell your product. This is a technologically savvy group; get on the Internet, and communicate via e-mail.

insure success. Personally invite as many people as you can to get involved. Make a list of pastors, pastoral associates, priests, and lay leaders who will support your work in young adult ministry. Keep them informed about your ministry and what you are accomplishing. They can be persuasive persons for you and advocates for young adult ministry.

12. Learn to "sell" your success.

For many reasons, the importance of young adult ministry is misunderstood. In many dioceses, young adults continue to be the most neglected age group in the church. Few parishes have a specific ministry for young adults, and diocesan resources are minimal. If you are fortunate enough to be working in young adult ministry, keep good records of your programs, the number of people you are reaching, and the events that are successful. This will be the foundation on which to build your case for continuing and strengthening young adult ministry. Share the data with your bishop, diocesan leaders, and pastors. Not only will they see the effectiveness of your work, but also you will be educating them about programmatic responses to the needs of young adults.

Hints for the Leaders
of a Diocesan Young Adult Ministry Office

1. Find some mentors.

Who are the people you can go to for advice, to test ideas, and to get support in the work you are doing? Make a list of those people, and try to connect with them on a regular basis. They will help to renew your energy and keep things in perspective. If you cannot sit with them, call them or e-mail them. There are people with wisdom they would be happy to share. Let people feed you.

If you are a lay person working in the church, either as a staff member or a volunteer, look for mentors who also work with or have a fondness for young adults in the church. Seek out parish leaders who have a passion for this age group. There may not be many young adult ministers, but there certainly are others who work with or at least are in touch with young adults. Connect with religious education directors, those responsible for RCIA, ministers who are young adults themselves, anyone from whose wisdom and experience you might benefit. Networking with others who can be supportive is important. Do not allow yourself to be isolated. Know who you can call for support and who will genuinely take an interest in the work you are doing.

2. Dream big, think small, go slow.

Sr. Margaret O'Brien, former director of young adult ministry for the Diocese of Rockville Centre, New York, coined this formula and used it very effectively. *Dream big:* It all starts with the dream of what can be. What would you like a ministry to young adults to look like some day? Dream about it, think about it, and write it down. *Think small:* Where do you want to begin? Convert the dream into manageable pieces. What single program or activity is immediately achievable and will establish a good beginning? *Go slow:* Take your time. The biggest problem is that people try to do too much too soon. That often leads to frustration among the leaders, ineffective programs, and less than anticipated participation.

3. You can't do everything, and you're not going to be good at everything.

Effective ministry is built on the ability to respond to people's needs while activating your own dreams and talents. Often that means asking others to help. No one person has the talent or skill to respond to all of the needs of young adults. Know clearly what you like to do and where your gifts lie. Surround yourself with people who can help you get the job done, especially in those areas where you do not excel. Rely on volunteers when needed. They have a great deal to offer.

4. Maintain your own personal and spiritual growth.

Where do you get fed? What keeps you going? Who helps to sustain your vision? Where do you go for wisdom? The answer to those questions is going to be different for everyone. Do whatever you need to do to stay healthy and spiritually alive.

5. Connect with other diocesan agencies and offices.

There are other diocesan offices that can be helpful to your work in young adult ministry. Consider joint efforts between your office and the following: Ministry in Higher Education, Family Ministry, Office for Catechesis, Ethnic Ministry Office, Vocations Office, Office for Divine Worship, Peace and Justice Office, etc. Are there other dioceses in your area that have young adult ministry programs? It could be helpful to network with other diocesan leaders in young adult ministry.

Chapter 11

Young Adult Ministry, Chicago-Style

The Young Adult Ministry Office for the Archdiocese of Chicago has been evolving for more than two decades. Begun in August 1977 as a very new part-time ministry, it became a full-time ministry and archdiocesan office on July 1, 1985. We have already shared the vision and goals of a ministry to young adults on a diocesan level. In this chapter we wish to share some of the programs and activities that have developed from our vision and goals—the results of over twenty years of hard work and learned-from mistakes.

General Publicity

Any young adult who contacts our office is added to our mailing list. We send a welcoming letter with general information about the opportunities our office provides and publicity about events occurring within the next several months. On the next few pages we have reproduced the general publicity statement, which gives an idea of the scope of the programs offered.

Young Adult Ministry is the Catholic Church's outreach to women and men, married and single, in their twenties and thirties. Young Adult Ministry provides young adults opportunities to gather with peers, share values, explore issues, and search for meaning in life. Here are some of the ways we might be of assistance to you, your friends, and your parish.

Our free quarterly newsletter is the main communication vehicle provided by the Young Adult Ministry Office. In March, the newsletter presents information about our annual young adult conference, **FOCUS.** In June, it contains details about **Theology-on-Tap,** our four-week speaker and discussion series hosted by parishes throughout the Archdiocese of Chicago (Cook and Lake Counties). Our publication has a circulation of over twenty-eight thousand young adults. We would be happy to add you and any other young adults to our mailing list—just send names and addresses to: Young Adult Ministry, 711 W. Monroe, Chicago, IL 60661 or yam@yamchicago.org. We also have a monthly on-line "e-letter," complete with updates on what's happening throughout the Chicagoland area. Just give us your e-mail address, and we will keep you informed.

The Young Adult Ministry Office has become aware of the growing need to assist young adults with an awareness of the Catholic tradition and how our faith plays an important role in our daily lives. We are not "Sunday" Catholics. We are people striving to see our faith as an integral part of each day and each human experience. We also are aware that many young adults did not receive much religious formation during their school years. Now with more life experience, we are seeking meaning and understanding. In other words, we're not kids any longer. Our faith should grow as we do. To assist in ongoing religious development, the Young Adult Ministry Office provides a number of opportunities to explore the Catholic faith.

- **Theology-on-Tap:** This four-week speaker and discussion program is co-sponsored by the Young Adult Ministry Office and over sixty parishes. Held every summer, it begins in July at various locations throughout the Archdiocese of Chicago and the Dioceses of Joliet and Rockford in Illinois, the Diocese of Gary, Indiana, and the Archdiocese of Milwaukee, Wisconsin. The series ends with a special Mass at Holy Name Cathedral and a picnic with Cardinal George on a Sunday afternoon in August. Theology-on-Tap has been hosted every summer since 1981. Over those first twenty years, more than 250 speakers have addressed pertinent issues at 146 parishes. Conservatively, over 20,000 young adults have participated.

For information, please contact us at 312-466-9473,
yam@yamchicago.org, or www.yamchicago.org.

- **FOCUS:** Held on a Saturday afternoon and evening in May, this one-day conference has become one of the largest gatherings of Catholic young adults anywhere in the United States! Over one thousand young adults come to enjoy a keynote talk, two or three rounds of workshops, Mass, dinner, and a party. The sixty workshops include topics on relationships, faith, personal growth, and work issues.

- **Young Adult Weekend Retreat:** A retreat is a great gift to give yourself. It's a weekend away from the routine of life and a chance to rest and reflect on what's important. It's also an excellent opportunity to meet and spend quality time with your peers. The retreat directors, chosen for their special relationship with young adults, provide good input. The Young Adult Ministry Office sponsors two retreats yearly, one every fall, and one every winter.

- **Catholicism Revisited:** People often leave Theology-on-Tap looking for more. This seminar, held on several Saturdays in winter, is for those who are interested in exploring theology, church history, and Catholic practices in greater depth. Highly talented presenters are invited to address specific topics and answer questions related to the rich traditions of the Catholic faith and how they work in our lives.

- **Prayer & Scripture:** In this winter series of talks, we address some of the "tools" of Catholicism. One evening a week for six consecutive weeks young adults gather to take a good look at various types of prayer and the way Catholics approach Scripture.

- **Relationships! What a Trip!** At this Saturday afternoon event, held in winter at various sites, we take a look at the relationships of our lives. The event includes a keynote talk, discussion on topics raised by participants, and small group sharing. Topics we have addressed include communication, finding the right person, dating, marriage, dealing with the pain of broken relationships, and keeping commitments.

- **Pearls of Wisdom** and **More Than We Seem:** The Young Adult Ministry Office hosts a number of programs on spirituality. **Pearls of Wisdom** is an afternoon dedicated to spiritual nourishment for women; **More Than We Seem** is a gathering for young adult men. Both programs focus on who we are as daughters and sons of God and the unique gifts we have been given to share.

- **YACHT Club (Young Adult Catholics Hanging Together):** once a month young adults gather at various restaurants throughout the city and suburbs for a guest speaker, good conversation, and a meal. Come and meet some people over dinner, while focusing on an important issue. For specific dates, times, and places of the next meeting nearest you, please call us (312-466-9473) or visit our website (www.yamchicago.org).

- **Transitions—A Day to Explore Movement in Your Work Life:** This afternoon workshop includes a keynote talk and opportunities to discuss with your peers various aspects of work. Past topics have included: What Do I Want to Be Doing in Five Years? Faith in the Workplace; Dealing with Difficult Co-Workers; Can I Do What I Really Want to Do? Moving to Nonprofit Work; Becoming an Entrepreneur; Does This Job Fit Who I Am? Is There More to Me Than Work? Improving Networking Ability; and Balancing Work, Relationships, and Faith.

- **You're As Good As You Feel—A Day on Healthy Living:** Just how fit are you? We hear so much about healthy living, eating right, exercising, and finding other ways to get rid of stress. Health professionals come and present information and insights about maintaining good physical health.

- **Annual Young Adult Co-ed Volleyball Tournament:** Every winter, on the weekend before the Superbowl, parishes get their teams together and come out to play recreational volleyball. The goal is to meet new people, learn what other groups are doing, and have some fun.

- **Good Conversation:** Sometimes there is a need to talk things out—nothing fancy, just a *good conversation* about things that happen in life. Fr. John Cusick and Ms. Kate DeVries are available simply to chat. Give us a call at 312-466-9473. We also refer people to counselors with special skills.

In addition to keeping you informed through our quarterly newsletter and offering the events listed above, we are available to help you on an **individual basis.** Here are a number of other ways people have taken advantage of the Young Adult Ministry Office.

> **You're invited to join approximately 500 other young adults every month for worship and a continental breakfast.**
>
> ## *Young Adult Sunday Mass*
>
> The First Sunday of Every Month All Year
> **Old St. Patrick's Church, 11:15 a.m.**
> Adams and Des Plaines, Chicago
>
> Take any expressway to the Kennedy Expressway. Exit at Monroe Street. Go east one block to Des Plaines. Turn right on Des Plaines and go south one block to Adams. Park in any lot across the street from the church.

- **Where young adults gather...** We direct people to places where young adults gather for worship, where parish young adult groups are meeting, and where other young adult activities are taking place.

- **Where and when you can volunteer...Volunteers-in-Action** is a referral network for young adults looking to do something for others. Michelle Doyle, our volunteer coordinator (and a volunteer herself), can connect you with an organization in need of your time and talent. To speak with Michelle, leave a message for her at the Young Adult Office.

- Another way to share your time and talent is to **volunteer in the Young Adult Ministry Office.** If you want to meet some great people while providing a wonderful service to your peers, please call Kate at 312-466-9473. Some young adults come in to help on a weekly basis; others twice a month; others work on specific projects as often as their schedules allow.

For People with Special Interests...

- **Small Faith Groups:** Throughout the city and suburbs, young adults are meeting in groups of eight to ten, twice a month to discuss faith issues. This is an opportunity to meet with your peers for stimulating conversation about how God is at work in our lives.

- **Young Married Couples Groups:** These groups respond to the desire of young married couples to share their faith with other couples. In each group, ten to twelve couples come together for lively conversation about concerns related to today's marriages. The groups meet once a month on a Friday evening in the home of one of the participants.

- **Separated/Divorced Support Group:** We have created support groups for young adults who have experienced divorce or marital separation. If you are interested in connecting with others who have experienced this pain, please let us know.

- **Grief Support Group:** We have established groups for young adults who are working through the pain and emptiness caused by the death of a loved one. If you have recently experienced the loss of a loved one and would find value in gathering with your peers who have "been there," please call us at 312-466-9473.

- **Jewish-Catholic Couples Group:** This very successful group has been meeting since 1988. Its purpose is to help people who come from these two great religious traditions to deal with the concerns and questions related to such a relationship. Many different types of couples come to the monthly meetings: married with and without children, engaged, dating, and couples curious to see if such a relationship can work. For details, please call Dan and Abbe at . . .

For You, Your Peers, and Your Parish . . .

Finally, the Young Adult Ministry Office is able to help you and your parish several different ways. Often young adults feel isolated or overlooked in their parishes. Two comments are heard over and over again: "Where are the people my age on Sunday?" and "There never seems to be anything directed to young adults in our parish." Interestingly, parish staff people often have two similar comments: "We don't see many young adults at Mass on Sunday in our parish" and "It's hard to plan for our young adults because they are really not around the parish." It seems like a vicious circle. The Young Adult Ministry Office can offer help to parishes in four specific ways:

1. **Meeting with the parish staff to discuss ways of working with young adults.** On occasion the Young Adult Ministry Office has the opportunity of entering into good conversation with an entire parish staff or those on the staff who express an interest in young adults. The purpose of this meeting is to offer concrete suggestions about effective ways of inviting and integrating young adults into the life and activity of the parish.

2. **Planning a parish young adult group.** Would you and others you know be interested in developing a young adult group in your parish? We would be

happy to work with you. Throughout the last few years, we have learned a lot about young adults, their relationship to the church, and their interest in groups and activities. Based on the success and failures of other young adult groups, we are able to share practical suggestions about things to do and things to avoid doing. We offer leadership training annually to help people interested in developing a group.

3. **Planning a dialogue group.** Some people are looking for ongoing conversation with their peers. This type of group isn't limited to people from a particular parish; it can be established among friends, classmates, people you meet at young adult events, others in your building, etc. It's an opportunity to have a serious discussion with others on a regular basis. The Young Adult Ministry Office can offer you suggestions for creating and maintaining a dialogue group (see Appendix D, "Creating and Maintaining a Dialogue Group").

4. **Hosting young adult activities.** Do you think your parish would like to be a host site for Theology-on-Tap, Catholicism Revisited, a day on relationships or spirituality, or a small faith group? The value of hosting a program is that people come together for a few meetings—and it's over, short, and to the point. The Young Adult Ministry Office is always interested in co-sponsoring young adult activities with parishes. Ask your parish staff if they might be interested. Then give us a call: **312-466-9473.**

Young Adult Ministry Office
711 W. Monroe, Chicago, IL 60661
phone: 312-466-9473 fax: 312-466-9474
e-mail: yam@yamchicago.org
http://www.yamchicago.org

Rev. John C. Cusick   *Ms. Katherine F. DeVries*

A Closer Look

To provide a better understanding of the events we offer and the way we present them, we will explain some of them here in greater detail. A word of caution: We are constantly asked, "Tell me what programs work for young adults." There is no guarantee that any of these programs will "work." Programs do not make young adult ministry effective. People do. We cannot emphasize enough that it is always *people before programs*. In other words, it is not as much about what you do as the people you gather to do it.

Theology-on-Tap

Theology-on-Tap is a four-week summer speaker and discussion series exclusively for young adults. It is an opportunity for parishes to gather their young adults regionally for a speaker, conversation, and good theology. One parish in cooperation with other parishes in the area hosts the program.

Theology-on-Tap began in June of 1981 at St. James Parish in Arlington Heights, Illinois. It was a response to a conversation between a parish priest and a young man from the parish who was graduating from college. That man was looking beyond his last few months of college to the "real world." He was facing a career and wondering about the future. He was concerned about his personal identity and finding meaning in life. "Will I be more than my job? What will it mean to fall in love? Where does God fit in all this? What does it mean to be Catholic?" Theology-on-Tap was designed for young adults asking these and similar questions.

The year 2001 marked the twenty-first consecutive summer that parishes in the Archdiocese of Chicago hosted Theology-on-Tap. The program has become a means for parishes to focus time, attention, and

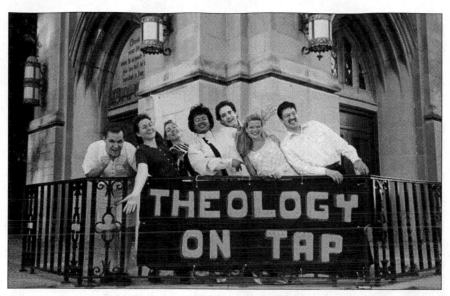

The Theology-on-Tap planning committee from St. Gertrude Parish had a great deal of fun inviting their peers to participate in the four-week speaker and discussion series.

resources on one of the most overlooked groups of people in the parish, people in their twenties and thirties. Theology-on-Tap is also an excellent opportunity to make those younger parishioners feel welcome and at home in their church.

Every summer beginning the week after the Fourth of July, Theology-on-Tap happens on Sunday, Monday, Tuesday, and Wednesday evenings in various parts of the Archdiocese of Chicago and surrounding dioceses. Each session lasts two hours, once a week, over the course of the four weeks.

Parishes that will participate in the program are chosen based on their interest in gathering young adults, ability to assemble a strong committee of young adults to host it, and geographical location. After a parish agrees to host Theology-on-Tap, we work with them to create a plan for direct personal invitation to their young adults and those in the surrounding area. We carefully walk their committee members through the manual, which contains everything they will need to know to make the program successful. We coordinate their speakers and topics and do archdiocesan-wide publicity to promote the program. They extend a more

The Theology-on-Tap Manual

A Theology-on-Tap manual was written so that parishes, regions, and dioceses new to the program could learn from and build upon the success of previous Theology-on-Tap sessions. That manual, which is available for purchase, contains the following information:

- background and purpose
- a step-by-step planning guide
- the organizational structure
- information about the target group
- a strategy for effectively reaching young adults
- a "road map" from the point of view of a hosting committee member
- helpful hints for success
- a sample session
- sample letters and bulletin and pulpit announcements
- hints on hospitality
- lists of topics that have been addressed
- copies of the Theology-on-Tap logo.

We have done our best to share the wisdom of the past twenty-one years of hosting the program. We have also learned that those who follow the manual are successful; others may or may not be.

For details about obtaining the manual and for permission to host Theology-on-Tap (we hold the copyright), please contact the Young Adult Ministry Office, 312-466-9473.

personal invitation, create publicity for their area, arrange all the details necessary for a successful program, and host the program each of the four nights.

At the end of the four weeks, all who have participated in the program are invited to join us for Mass with the cardinal archbishop at Holy Name Cathedral, followed by a lawn party at the cardinal's residence.

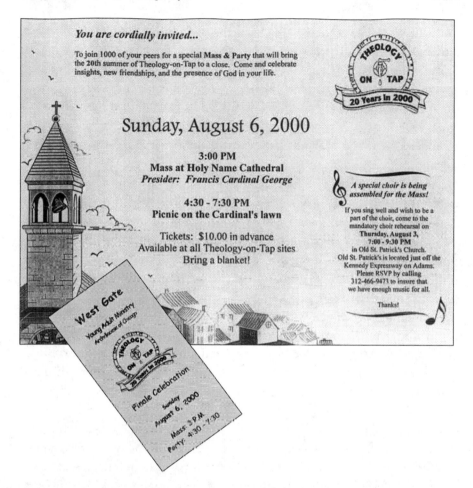

The Theology-on-Tap Mass is held the Sunday after the last Wednesday session, and begins at 3:00 p.m. It is a phenomenal celebration, with special care given to incorporating the rich diversity of the church in Chicago. Again, we do our best to put forth good preaching, good music, and good hospitality. We hand-pick talented instrumentalists, lectors, and cantors to share their gifts. With the exception of the clergy who concelebrate, all of the ministers (ushers, greeters, Eucharistic ministers, gift bearers, and altar servers) are young adults. To walk into such a glorious space as Holy Name Cathedral and realize that almost everyone present is a young adult is a powerful experience. It is not often that young adults enjoy being surrounded by so many of their peers at worship. The music includes a variety of styles and languages, and we prepare a worship aid.

At all of the Theology-on-Tap sessions, we invite those with a gift for singing to participate in the choir. Approximately sixty young adult women and men sing, and we personally invite about twelve instrumentalists and several cantors from various parishes. They rehearse for two hours the Thursday evening between their last talk and the Mass and then come an hour early that Sunday. Under the care of a gifted director, they sound fabulous. As an extra expression of hospitality, free day care is provided during the Mass for the children of our young adult parents.

After Mass, everyone is invited to continue the celebration at the lawn party at the cardinal's residence. That party consists of a buffet-dinner, dancing to a DJ, and games. All of the hosting sites sell tickets for the party at every session. Tickets cost $10 each, and, with the help of a reduced rate from the caterer, cover the expenses of the event (our goal is always to break even). The party lasts from 4:30 to 7:30 p.m. Cardinal George and the bishops who join us from neighboring dioceses work hard at connecting personally with as many young adults as possible. It is not often that people of any age have a bishop or cardinal's undivided attention. Additionally, the bishops and cardinal benefit greatly from exposure to the energy, gratitude, concerns, pain, and joy of this segment of their flock. It is at this finale celebration that we see best that we are one body in Christ.

There is a financial obligation on the part of the parishes hosting Theology-on-Tap. It costs $800 to host the program. The speaker stipend is $125 for each session. The remaining $300 is spent on refreshments, publicity, and postage. We give each parish several manuals, which include pages of logos, sample flyers, bulletin announcements, etc. The local parish does publicity for the young adults in their area after we send out a mailing to everyone on our list. Our mailing presents complete details of who is speaking where and when for all the participating parishes (approximately sixty) along with directions to each site and speaker biographies. Again, people purchase their own party tickets, which are sold at each hosting parish. Everything is local. All of our expenses have been brokered out to parishes and the participants who choose to attend the closing celebration.

Parishes do not charge people to attend Theology-on-Tap; it is our primary form of evangelization to young adults. Usually, parishes sponsor Theology-on-Tap as part of their adult religious education programs. Either one parish can pay the entire cost of the program for the area, or several

---

Where are you?

Make sure places are easy to find! For Theology-on-Tap we have a map to each site, along with directions. Post signs leading from the street or corner of your property to the meeting room. Many people in this generation have been away for a while and are afraid to walk in the door. Posted signs are an indication that this is a welcoming place to be. Don't let people get frustrated and leave because they couldn't find the right room. And don't assume anyone knows the location of a room by its name ("Golden Hall" means nothing to most people). Make sure that a stranger from out of town could find you easily.

---

supporting parishes can divide the amount. When enough young adults participate in the program, the expense for this solid catechesis and a good Catholic experience is minimal. For the parishes that cannot afford the program, we do some creative brainstorming. How about a fundraiser or corporate sponsorship to help them with expenses? Instead of ending the discussion when they say, "We can't afford it," ask, "How can we afford it?" This is our approach to finances: If it is of value, how can we make it happen? When parishes have the desire but cannot afford the program, we encourage them to go ahead, and we find benefactors to assist them.

FOCUS Conference

FOCUS is an opportunity for young adults to **FOCUS** on Family, Others, Church, Unity, and Self.

There is strength in numbers. We decided to create a one-day young adult event in order to bring together lots of young adult people. Very often Catholic young adults feel like a minority in their own church. They see few people their age in attendance at church events, including weekend Mass. Our one-day event is a real happening. There is an energy and

FOCUS conference schedule

9:30–Noon	Registration
10:00–5:45	Day Care
9:30–6:00	Book Sales
10:15–11:30	Preconference Workshops
12:00–12:15	Opening Prayer
12:15–1:00	Keynote Address
1:00–1:50	Lunch Break
2:00–3:30	Workshop I
4:00–5:30	Workshop II
6:00–7:15	Mass
7:30–8:30	Dinner
8:30–11:00	Party

an excitement from the time people walk through the door in the late morning until the last song is played—sometimes early the next morning! We decided to create an event for young adults that would allow them to experience their faith positively in their head, their heart, their soul, and their gut. We provide a keynote presentation that inspires, workshops filled with insights, live music throughout the day, festive worship, and dinner and a party that celebrates life in abundance.

FOCUS is an annual conference planned by and hosted for young adults. The conference was modeled on the young adult conference created by the Young Adult Ministry Office in the Archdiocese of Los Angeles. We host FOCUS on a Saturday in May, from noon until 11 p.m. The day begins with a keynote talk, followed by two rounds of workshops. The workshops are divided into four areas: the largest and most popular is relationships. The second largest is faith issues, and the third is work issues. The fourth area includes issues of personal development, such as balancing work, faith, and other aspects of life. Because so many young adults have requested a third round of workshops, we now offer

Music for the FOCUS conference Mass is provided by young adults interested in sharing their gifts.

"preconference sessions" that begin at 10:15 a.m. for no additional cost. Just over half our participants register for a preconference session. One of those preconference sessions is always a "Meet and Greet, Mix and Match" workshop, made up of enjoyable icebreakers. It's a great way for people who come alone to get connected. After all, one of the most often expressed needs of young adults is to meet good people. That's how our FOCUS conference begins, and that spirit continues throughout the day.

The keynote talk begins after the opening prayer at noon. Next is lunch, followed by the two rounds of workshops. After the workshops, we have a Mass together with a volunteer choir. As we do with Theology-on-Tap, we host a choir rehearsal the Thursday before the event, usually with fifty or so voices and about a dozen instrumentalists. Then we have a buffet style dinner and a party. It is a day packed with activities for young adults with plenty of time to interact with one another, meet new people, and enjoy some quality input.

> ### *Selecting speakers*
>
> Make sure your speakers meet two criteria: they have to have something worthwhile to say, and they have to be able to say it well (they have to have a "good act"). Some speakers who are the best "entertainers" do not have much to say. Conversely, other speakers' content is outstanding, but they are incredibly lifeless and boring. The best speakers offer a combination of strong content and exciting delivery. The speakers you choose are a reflection not only of your ministry to young adults, but also a reflection of the image of the Catholic Church you wish to present to young adults.

The first year we hosted FOCUS, we had five committees working to plan the event: Publicity, Workshops, Liturgy, Registration, and Social. Now that the conference has grown to be one of the most significant gatherings of young adult Catholics in the country, we have expanded to fifteen committees. They are listed below.

FOCUS 2001 Committees

- *Administrative Support:* Handles all aspects of the conference that do not fall within the responsibilities of a specific committee. Members of this committee are "on call" to help as needed and support all other committees.

- *Advertising:* Organizes and implements the sale of ads for the FOCUS conference book; solicits support for underwriting parts of the day.

- *Computer Support:* Handles all aspects for which computers are needed, including registration, reports needed by committees, website design, and e-mail publicity.

- *Day Care:* Arranges for the care of children of FOCUS attendees throughout the day.

- *Finance:* Pays bank registration fees and all FOCUS bills, oversees committee budgets, completes final attendance and final finance reports.

- *Ethnic Outreach:* Invites Hispanic, Polish, African-American, and Asian young adults to participate in FOCUS; promotes an ethnic presence in all aspects of the conference by direct personal invitation, suggesting and inviting speakers and publicity to various communities and organizations.

- *Liturgy:* Coordinates opening prayer service and weekend liturgy; works with artists to create the FOCUS 2001 banner for all participants to sign; arranges for the banner to be put out on tables, signed, and hung during Mass.

- *Operations:* Assures that all aspects of the conference run smoothly, including set-up, posting signs, day care facilities, providing for physically challenged guests, etc.

- *Publications:* Produces the newsletter with complete details about the conference and the conference book that will be distributed to all participants.

- *Publicity:* Publicizes the conference to all young adults throughout the Archdiocese of Chicago through local media, diocesan communications, visits to parish young adult groups, pulpit announcements, etc.

- *Raffle/Fund Raising:* Solicits goods, sends thank-you letters to sponsors, prepares publicity for the newsletter, pulls winning tickets at the conference, distributes prizes to winners.

- *Registration:* Coordinates preregistration, day of registration, and complete final attendance report.

- *Social:* Provides a social and festive atmosphere throughout the day, by decorating the conference site, arranging morning refreshments, planning entertainment (morning, during lunch, dinner, and party), coordinating lunch, dinner, and the party.

- *Volunteers:* Maintains contact with the people who offer to help run the conference, recruits volunteers, assigns them to committees, and does follow-up to insure that all who offer to help are enjoying their committee work.

- *Workshops:* Plans workshops, invites and confirms speakers, coordinates introducers for speakers, distributes evaluation forms, prepares speaker folder and name badges.

People are personally invited onto committees based on their talent, interests, available time, and leadership skills. Often committee members from a previous year are promoted to be one of two or three committee chairs for the upcoming year. Last year's committee chairs who worked well are invited back but given the option of helping in another capacity. Some young adults accept the challenge of improving upon their work of the previous year; others take on a new challenge and join another committee. Either way, the conference is enriched by their gifts.

Planning a diocesan conference is a huge undertaking. Make sure that you have several key young adults to help you manage the committees. We call them our "administration committee," and we delegate to them as much as possible. A monthly planning meeting with all committees represented should be enough to keep you informed, keep it exciting, troubleshoot where necessary, and affirm the many gifts that are being shared. Everyone interested is invited to those planning meetings. The administration committee can set the agenda and invite people. Then the main role of the staff becomes one of support. Whenever committees need more volunteers, decisions must be made, official letters or phone calls have to be handled, or there is a major hurdle to overcome, the staff can intervene. The responsibility of the staff is to offer the vision for the task, to extend hospitality, and to pass out "Way to Go's." Trust is required. They are adults, and they will get the job done. What falls through the cracks, the administration people will catch as they oversee the big picture.

Young Adult Retreats

The first young adult retreat that our Young Adult Ministry Office hosted was by invitation only. The goal was to break a stereotype of young adults who usually came to retreats and what they come seeking. Ninety personal letters of invitation were sent out. Thirty-five people, many of whom had never been on an adult retreat, enjoyed a wonderful weekend. An unexpected comment was heard frequently as people left the retreat house: "Thanks for inviting me. I wouldn't have come if you hadn't." Now we fill the retreat house with eighty participants for each of our two annual retreats. It is not unusual for the retreat house to have a waiting list for the upcoming young adult retreat.

Our retreats last from Friday evening till Sunday at 2:00 p.m. The topics for the retreats come directly from what we hear young adults say they

Retreat schedule

Friday

7:00 p.m.	Registration
8:00 p.m.	Orientation, introductions
9:00 p.m.	Conference I
10:00 p.m.	Evening prayer

Saturday

8:00 a.m.	Prayer for Early Risers
8:30 a.m.	Breakfast
9:30 a.m.	Conference II
Noon	Midday Prayer
12:30 p.m.	Lunch
1:30 p.m.	Conference III
3:30 p.m.	Free time
5:30 p.m.	Dinner
7:00 p.m.	Conference IV
8:30 p.m.	Reconciliation Service
9:30 p.m.	Party

Sunday

8:30 a.m.	Breakfast
9:30 a.m.	Conference V
11:00 a.m.	Weekend Mass
12:30 p.m.	Lunch & Departure

want or need. We sometimes build around the theme of an outstanding speaker. Usually, one of us is present to help preach and lead prayer.

At every retreat, we gather a group of people for forty hours. Throughout the weekend, there are five conferences and five prayer services. We allow ample time for quiet reflection, input, small group sharing, and large group sharing. The small group sharing is important; young adults mention it, together with weekend Mass, as what they enjoy most on the retreats we host.

We have prepared a handout called "Eleven Ways to Use This Retreat Effectively" to encourage young adults to set their own agenda for the weekend (see Appendix E).

Many people who attend will have never been on a retreat before. Let them know what to expect. Lay it all out on Friday evening. Allow people to get to know one another. We begin every retreat by asking people to introduce themselves and share whatever they choose about why they came. The rewards of that sharing will be evident, as people connect throughout the weekend by what was said on Friday evening.

Young adults on the retreat do not have to attend every session and do not have to join a discussion group. If they want to, they are welcome, but it is not required. Make sure you emphasize the *adult*, not the *young*. Respect people's individuality and freedom. We are not a grown-up teen club, and there are no compulsory exercises. We put material out so they can enter into dialogue with one another or go off and be by themselves. It is always their choice.

Organizing and leading a young adult retreat can be a great challenge. Young adults often express totally opposite needs during a retreat. Some express the desire for good conversation. Others want more personal and quiet time. People choose how and with whom they wish to spend their time.

Provide a printed agenda and lot of handouts that participants can refer to in the future. You never know when they will go back and use them again. We jot down and type out the comments we hear in the large group on Sunday morning. We include them in a letter to all participants two weeks after the retreat. We thank them for their presence and remind them of the Good News of the weekend. It helps to keep the spirit of the retreat alive a while longer.

During the retreat, young adults will begin asking for the names, addresses, and phone numbers of other participants. Though we have that information, we do not share it. Not everyone wants their information shared. Before leaving the retreat house on Sunday morning, we invite people to add their names, addresses, phone numbers, and e-mail addresses to a page provided for that purpose. We type up that list and distribute it to all retreatants.

Many young adults are looking for opportunities to learn more about Catholicism and ways of growing deeper spiritually. Talks based on young adult concerns and questions can provide such opportunities.

Teaching the Faith: Catechesis

Learning more about spirituality, faith, and the Catholic tradition has become very important for young adults. As a matter of fact, in the hierarchy of expressed needs, learning more about their faith ranks right behind concerns about relationships. This spiritual hunger is reflected in both religious and secular data revealing that this generation of young adults is in fact a spiritually hungry one. Consequently, much of our work now focuses on formulating catechetical programs designed to help young adults explore their faith and feed that spiritual hunger.

Many young adults say that they know little about their faith, that they received minimal religious formation during the earlier years of their lives. Now as adults they want to know what their Catholic tradition is about and the ways it can be applied to their daily lives.

Earlier in this chapter we discussed Theology-on-Tap, which is our primary catechetical program. Here are some others.

Catholicism Revisited is subtitled "Perhaps It's That Time in Your Life to Re-Examine Your Religious Roots." It is a program designed to look at

What's in a name?

Name every program you offer, and design a logo for it. If you name it, you own it. When people see the logo, they'll remember it.

CATHOLICISM REVISITED
PERHAPS IT'S THAT TIME IN YOUR LIFE TO RE-EXAMINE YOUR RELIGIOUS ROOTS

YACHT CLUB — Young Adult Catholics Hanging Together

Prayer & Scripture

Relationships! What a Trip!
A Day to Look at Where Our Personal Relationships Have Been and Where They Are Going

Transitions
A Day to Explore Movements in Your Work Life.

A strategy for hosting programs

The first time we hosted these events, we did so at our office. After an initial success, we co-hosted future programs at a parish with a strong young adult group. Then the local parishes took on the responsibility. We call the local parish and say, "How about we do a day on relationships in March?" It takes our work, localizes it in a parish, and gives the parish an opportunity to offer an event for young adults. We help to deliver people by publicizing the event in our newsletter, in our e-letter, and at our young adult First Sunday of the Month Mass.

some important dimensions of Catholicism: historical moments; Scripture; beliefs; rituals, signs, and symbols; the sacraments, especially reconciliation and the Eucharist. We began Catholicism Revisited in response to young adults who enjoyed Theology-on-Tap but were looking for greater depth about their Catholic faith.

In response to the hunger young adults have expressed about how to pray and how to use Scripture, we created **PS—Prayer & Scripture.** Favorite topics include: Praying from the Experiences of Our Lives; Becoming a Praying Person— How to Get There; Meditation: Developing the Skill of Reflection; A Catholic Approach to Understanding Scripture; Reading Between the Lines—Unpacking the Symbols; If We Are Not Fundamentalists, What Are We? Language and Stories in the Bible; and Taking a Good Look at the Gospels.

The YACHT Club (Young Adult Catholics Hanging Together) is an interesting adventure, where participants meet one evening a month in a local restaurant. After introductions and dinner together, a speaker addresses a relevant issue. Then people stay for faith-filled conversation.

For programs like **Pearls of Wisdom** (women's spirituality), **More Than We Seem** (men's spirituality), **Relationships! What a Trip!** and **Transitions** (a day on work), we invite young adults to come together on a Saturday afternoon. Mindful of young adult schedules, we try never to offer anything before noon on Saturday! (FOCUS preconference sessions are our one exception, and that is by popular demand.) Registration for these afternoon programs begins at noon, and they run from 1:00 p.m.

until 6:00 p.m. Whenever possible, we end with Mass for participants. Each of the workshops has a main presenter (often a young adult; sometimes a team of young adults) to provide food for thought, but a great deal of time is spent in small groups. We have found that young adults have much wisdom to share with their peers.

Charging a $6 to $10 registration fee allows us to pay speakers, provide refreshments, and cover our publicity costs. A team of volunteers is usually responsible for organizing the details of the program.

The Young Adult Mass the First Sunday of Every Month

On the first Sunday of every month, young adults in our archdiocese are invited to the 11:15 a.m. Mass at Old St. Patrick's Church. This is not a special Mass just for young adults, but a regularly scheduled Mass with a special invitation to young adults. People come from throughout the archdiocese and beyond for this spirit-filled Mass. The church that hosts the Mass is centrally located and easily accessible via expressway and public transportation. All the liturgical ministers—the greeters, ushers, lectors, gift bearers, and Eucharistic ministers—are young adults. We have two volunteers whose mission is to invite their peers into ministerial positions for that Mass. Each young adult is personally contacted, given specific information, and appropriately trained. After each "first Sunday" Mass, those liturgical ministers will receive a personal thank-you note for their help.

We do our best to provide quality worship, complete with good preaching, good hospitality, and good music. Following the Mass, all women and men in their twenties and thirties are invited to attend a continental breakfast. This has become a regular opportunity to meet people and recruit more volunteers for the work of young adult ministry. For those who are with us for the first time, one of us hosts a "first timers table." That gathering is an opportunity to meet newcomers, introduce them to one another, give them a quick look at what young adult ministry can offer them, add them to our mailing list, and learn other ways we might be helpful to them. The first timers table also encourages those who have come alone to attend the breakfast. Our goal is always this: although you may come in knowing no one, you will not leave knowing no one. We also now have hospitality people roaming the breakfast room looking for people who are standing alone. They converse with them and introduce

Young married couples groups

For the young married couples groups, we invite six to eight interested couples to come together and form one group. They are asked to gather monthly for as many times as there are couples in the group. This six-to-eight session commitment is needed for continuity; group formation takes time. At the first meeting, participants brainstorm about topics they would like to discuss. Those are written down and become the agenda for the successive monthly meetings. Every couple takes responsibility for hosting one meeting, on the topic they choose from the agreed upon list. They open their home, prepare refreshments, and establish the format for the evening. Occasionally, an outside "expert" is invited to address the topic for the group, but usually the lead couple begins the conversation, and others make their contribution. One evening, on the topic "Keeping Romance in the Marriage," the couple set up a different romantic experience in each room of their home. Each couple began the night in a different room, and every fifteen minutes, for an hour and a half, the couples moved from one delightful event to the next. After the exercise, more creative ideas were shared. Inviting each couple (or each participant) to take responsibility for one meeting makes a great deal of sense. That way, no one leader is overburdened, and everyone experiences a leadership role.

It is important to have a definite beginning and ending time for each meeting as well as for the group itself. We suggest an hour and a half for each gathering and, as mentioned above, meeting for the same number of times as there are couples in the group. After each couple has hosted an evening, participants can decide to continue, take a break, or withdraw gracefully. In young adult ministry, we have learned the importance of beginning properly and ending gracefully.

them to others. We do our best to make them feel welcome, and it makes a huge difference.

There are many hidden values to this "first Sunday" young adult Mass. First, there is consistency. On the first Sunday of every month, all year long—even if it's New Year's Day—young adults in Chicago know that there is a place to worship and gather with their peers. Second, there is great

> ### *Begin with Sunday Mass*
>
> If you want to start an outreach to young adults in your diocese, find out where there already is a Sunday afternoon or evening Mass. That's where you'll find the young adults. If you run a program, piggy back it onto the end of that Mass. Begin with a place and a time where you know you are going to have the target group from which to draw.

strength in numbers; it is a powerful experience to see a church filled with young adults. Third, this is an excellent way to introduce many new people to our work. Typically forty to sixty people come to the first timers table. In other words, over a one-year period well over five hundred people are personally introduced to a church ministry designed specifically for them.

Leadership Training

Annually we offer leadership training to parish staff members and young adult leaders. Much of what we present is found in this text in Part Two. We emphasize the importance of hospitality throughout the entire training session. Since we have been at this work of young adult ministry for over two decades, we take a good look at what can go wrong in working with young adults, planning young adult activities, and developing a successful young adult program. We share from our experience what has worked.

Besides the annual training sessions (usually held on a Saturday) we also are available for similar leadership training at individual parishes and in various regions around the archdiocese. We have chosen not simply to put our leadership training manual in the mail for those who request information. We invite people seeking to develop a ministry to young adults to gather with us and review the leadership strategies step by step. This gives us the opportunity to meet them personally, to emphasize what we feel is most important, and to listen to their concerns. We do our best to shape the training for the local community and local congregation.

Listening Sessions

Our ministry to young adults has changed significantly over the years. This has occurred primarily through listening sessions where we have personally

> ## A great preacher series
>
> One of the most consistent needs of young adults is for good preaching. One church that attracts a large number of young adults to its Sunday evening Mass personally invites an outstanding guest preacher to join them once a month. Not only is the preaching very good, but the new voice adds to the experience of our Catholic faith.

invited a group of young adults to speak to us about their world, their needs and concerns, and their relationship to the Catholic Church. We have hosted similar listening sessions for young adults from particular ethnic and racial communities, young married couples, parents, etc. At these listening sessions, we also "test" some of our ideas for programs and other ways to reach young adults. These listening sessions have produced topics for the FOCUS conference and Theology-on-Tap. We have also learned much about the use of the Internet and e-mail newsletters from these listening sessions. Conducting a listening session is easy: personally invite a group of young people, state an issue or question, and just listen. They will tell you what they want, what they need, what they will attend, and what they won't attend. Often at the end of a listening session, people will be excited and even offer to help.

A young adult ministry that does the same things year after year is deadly. The ministers might be busy, but the ministry will become co-matose. Listening to young adults and re-creating our ministry with them will help to insure continued growth, genuine care, and positive responses.

Another form of listening is through written evaluations. We prepare

> ## The "faculty"
>
> Keep a file drawer of presenters who speak effectively to young adults. We call them our "faculty." The "faculty members" each get a file folder, complete with photo and curriculum vitae, details on how to reach them, a publicity page for each program in which they participate, and completed evaluation forms.

an evaluation form for every retreat, workshop, Theology-on-Tap talk, and other type of event that we host. We remind participants to fill them out at the end of the event and stress how important they are.

Your Turn

From what has been presented here, what are the most useful suggestions and strategies for your Catholic location?

- **Dream big:** write a paragraph describing what your vision for young adult ministry will look like five years from today.

- **Think small:** name ten key people and one guaranteed successful event upon which you wish to build your young adult ministry.

- **Go slow:** in chronological order, list your first five steps to develop your dream, find your key people, and create your first success.

Chapter 12

Volunteers

Church ministry is designed with volunteers in mind. Well over 90 percent of the people actively involved in parish life are volunteers: catechists, ministers of care, liturgical ministers, members of parish governance, to name but a few. Without volunteers, parish life would be greatly diminished.

This is true for young adult ministry as well. Without the presence and talent of young adult volunteers, young adult ministry would barely exist. We would like to share with you some ideas on inviting, nurturing, and training young adults to be effective volunteers.

In parish, regional, and diocesan young adult ministry, volunteers can assume two roles: within the Young Adult Ministry Office to keep the ministry moving forward, and beyond the office to help build a better world. Both roles are important; we will address each separately.

Volunteers in the Young Adult Ministry Office

Recruiting young adult volunteers is a skill. A director of a parish religious education program once said, "I never advertise in the bulletin for catechists, because then I'm stuck with whoever volunteers. As a result, I spend so much time reprogramming good will that I do not have the time to give to the people with the charism." How does she get the catechists she needs? "I go through the parent list after I've met and spent a bit of time with people. Then I decide who I think would be a good catechist. During the summer I call them and get to know them better. The people who understand who we are and the faith we are trying to share are the ones I personally invite into those positions. It's more work for me up front, but the payoff is well worth it." Only a handful of people will take the initiative and volunteer. Most people need to be asked and invited to help.

When you are creating your volunteer program, the following steps should prove helpful.

Recruiting and Supporting Volunteers

Step 1: Meet people and listen to them. When you meet young adults, talk to them about their interests, what they would like to see happen, and the gifts they have to share. Often you will hear people say, "I'm looking to get more involved." Make a list of the people you've met and their skills, interests, and hobbies. This information will be important when you personally invite them to participate as volunteers.

Step 2: Invite participation. As we mentioned above, we use the Jesus Method of Organizing to invite the participation of young adults (see p. 41). We use the same strategy to invite people to share their gifts and talents. Jesus' apostles were ordinary people he *hand picked* and *personally invited* to do God's work.

Take that list of people you've met and determine who might be supportive of current projects. Personally invite those young adults to volunteer their gifts. Chances are good that if you're looking for help in an area that interests them, they will consider volunteering. It's much harder to say "no" when you are personally invited.

When you speak with potential volunteers, be as specific as possible concerning the task, the time commitment required, and the completion date. Young adults are busy people. Asking for their support on short-term projects with a definite beginning and ending time usually will elicit a more positive response.

Step 3: Manage and support. The role of the staff person with regard to volunteers is to manage and support them. Meet with them to define the task, to obtain their input, and to make sure they understand what you want. As you become more comfortable with your volunteers, you will begin to know which projects require your continued involvement and which do not. Hand projects over whenever you can, and then check on progress periodically to see if you need to provide any additional information or help.

Step 4: Reward a job well done. There is no substitute for a "thank you." Who should receive a thank-you note? Is it time to host a volunteer

Interns

Many universities and colleges have programs with internship requirements. The students are skilled and ready to get to work, and we have much
work to be done. The time you spend training them will not only assist your
ministry, but will also prepare them to be ministers in their next situation.

thank-you dinner for an entire committee or larger group of volunteers?
How about sending flowers to someone who really went the extra mile?
A kind, grateful gesture will go a long way.

**Step 5: Be open to special volunteer projects and leaders ready to
make great things happen.** When you are approached with a good idea,
the answer should not be, "No, we don't have the time or money to do
this." Find a way to do the ordinary differently. Bring in a volunteer or a
team of volunteers to assume the role and see how far they can go with the
idea. We have "hosted" volleyball tournaments, a bicycling retreat, small
faith groups and other dialogue groups simply by letting those volunteers
who have the desire and skill put them together. We support the leaders
and publicize the event but have very little to do with the actual planning,
and it does not cost us any money. Young adults are talented and are
adults, and many are looking for a way to make a difference. It is our
responsibility to provide direction about where we can use their help. If
they are willing to take on the responsibility, everyone gains from the gift
of their talent, and they gain the experience and satisfaction of taking on
leadership in their church.

We use volunteers in our office for two types of tasks: day-to-day work
and specific projects.

Day-to-Day Work: Tasks include database edits, mailings, phone calls,
answering e-mail, website edits, preparing reports, running labels, copying
flyers, organizing, and the various other odd jobs that surface throughout
the week. We learned early that as our mailing list grew, so did the amount
of time it took to keep up with daily tasks. Although young adults were
more than willing to help us when we needed extra help, we weren't
always able to give them enough advance warning so they could work
it into their schedules. To address both concerns, we initiated a weekly

volunteer night. Having a consistent time and place allows more people to connect, because they can plan ahead. Every Thursday evening, between 5:30 and 9:30 p.m., people come in to help. They come as their schedules allow, to do whatever needs to be done. Everyone new to young adult ministry or who expresses an interest to "get involved" is personally invited to help any Thursday. By connecting with them in this day-to-day work, we get a sense of who should be invited to take on more responsibility.

Young adults who join this "Thursday night crew" come as soon as they can after work and usually stay for two hours. Some come every week, others once or twice a month. We operate on the principle: "Come whenever you can on Thursday. We will be here." We break for a simple meal at 7:00 p.m. That dinner break is a good opportunity to catch up on people's lives. Young adults would much rather come and meet people, enjoy a simple meal, and contribute to a cause than go home to an empty apartment or condo and eat alone. We are giving them an opportunity to connect socially while supporting their peers through church-sponsored activities. Good networking often happens during those volunteer hours.

Specific Projects: In addition to the day-to-day work, we invite young adults to assist with specific projects. The project people may choose to join us Thursday evenings, or they can pick a better day, time, and place to brainstorm, plan, and execute their tasks. Those projects have included the following:

- *Computer support:* creating and maintaining the website, preparing and distributing a monthly e-letter, managing computer hardware and software, generating computer reports as needed

- *Communications support:* writing and designing newsletters, event publicity, and general publicity

- *Telephone:* contacting inactive young adults or those you want to personally invite to an upcoming event

- *Development:* fund raising (events, raffles), writing grants, making direct appeals for financial support

- *Mass planning:* preparing music, inviting and coordinating liturgical ministers, creating worship aids

- *Committee work:* preparing for upcoming social, serious, spiritual, and service events

Whether for day-to-day work or for specific projects, several procedures should be in place:

- All volunteers sign in and out (see sample the Volunteer Sign-In Log below). At the end of each month, have one of your office volunteers tally the number of volunteers who participated and the total number of hours clocked. Such data can be helpful when meeting with your supervisors about next year's budget. Your efficient use of volunteers is saving the parish or diocese money.

Volunteer Sign-In Log

Thank You!

Date	Name	Time-In	Time-Out	Total Time	Project

- The first time anyone volunteers, that person completes the Volunteer Skills and Interests questionnaire (see the following page), which is placed in a Volunteer Notebook for future reference.

- A "To-Do" list of volunteer jobs is kept right next to the volunteer sign-in log. It is much easier to add jobs to the volunteer to-do list throughout the week than it is to come up with five jobs to be done when the volunteers arrive later that day.

- Volunteers who we know will get the job done are personally invited to handle big jobs. We give them the freedom to invite others they know to help. That keeps it enjoyable for the leaders and increases our volunteer pool. Also, be prepared to recruit others to help them if they request additional hands or wisdom on the project.

- For the big jobs we often invite two or three people to "co-chair" committees. That way, if one person has to drop out, we have one or two others to take up the slack. For larger events we add two or three more people than we will need; we call them our SWAT team (special weapons and tactics). They can troubleshoot as necessary or fill in for "no shows."

Volunteer Skills and Interests

Name _____ E-mail _____

Home Phone _____ Work Phone _____ Date of Birth _____

Date _____

✓ Please check the ways you are able to help. **Thank you!**

Artistic Skills
___ graphic arts
___ making signs
___ creating banners

Computer Work
___ data entry (we will train you)
___ e-mail correspondence (managing address book; sending information on upcoming programs)

Event Planning
___ brainstorming future topics and speakers
___ contacting potential speakers
___ committee work
___ planning liturgies
___ planning retreats

Finance
___ bookkeeping/accounting
___ creating expense reports

First Sunday of the Month Mass
(Old St. Patrick's Church)
___ greeter
___ Eucharistic minister
___ reader
___ usher
___ gift bearer

Fund Raising
___ contacting potential sponsors
___ helping coordinate a raffle

General Office Work
___ filing
___ typing
___ data entry
___ mailings
___ making phone calls
___ correspondence

Hospitality
___ greeting
___ helping to host a lunch or dinner
___ welcoming, bartending, setting up, cleaning up
___ contacting newcomers by phone

Languages (I can speak and write)
___ Spanish
___ Polish
___ Other

Newsletter
___ editing
___ writing
___ layout/graphic arts

Publicity/Communication
___ arranging press releases
___ contacting radio/TV
___ contact reports
___ creating flyers

Party Planning
___ arranging entertainment
___ coordinating games
___ creating a mixer
___ planning menu/contacting caterer
___ developing a party theme

Parish Contacts
___ I am connected at _____
church in _____
and can share information with my parish about upcoming young adult ministry events

Research and Planning
___ marketing strategies

Volunteers
___ contacting and scheduling volunteers

Other Gifts
___ photography
___ musician–instrument: _____
___ other _____

Please indicate how often you can help:
___ once a month
___ twice a month
___ two hours a week
___ call me when my skills are needed
___ call me to help with a special event
___ other _____

Is there a particular day of the week, time, or season of the year you are more available?
___ Monday
___ Tuesday   Best Time of Day:
___ Wednesday _____
___ Thursday
___ Friday   Good Months:
___ Saturday _____
_____

- When special talent is needed for which we have no one in mind, we ask for it at large gatherings. Usually several people come forward. This is how we got a web page and how we were able to transfer our database from one software program to another. We meet with these volunteers as a group to share our vision and establish a plan of action. One or two people at the meeting will surface as having the most experience; they are asked to take the lead.

- There should never be any guilt. If people let you down or get called out of town for the event or they cannot accomplish what they thought they could, graciously thank them for any work they have completed. Wish them well and tell them they are welcome to come in again when things ease up for them. They will feel guilty enough without us pushing the issue. Gracious hospitality will bring them back when their situation changes.

Here are some suggestions concerning the care of volunteers.

- Make every volunteer night fun, an opportunity to make people feel welcome and important. Keep looking for ways to keep it interesting and affirming.

- Teach volunteers the vision of young adult ministry. Before doing the work, teach them the way to do it. Leave nothing to chance. Give them a good experience of the Catholic Church, and they will share it.

- Respect their guidelines. Some will say, "I hate making phone calls!" or "I'm really good behind the scenes!" One doctor came to us and said, "I'll mop floors or stuff envelopes—just don't make me think!" If you are not respectful of them or their talent, they will justifiably leave and not return. If you are respectful, they may become some of your most loyal volunteers.

- Be sure there is plenty of food. Our volunteers bring food each Thursday evening. Often they order pizza; we always provide beverages. Our after-work food options have included sub sandwiches, cocktail meatballs, a veggie tray, grapes, pot luck meals, chips and salsa, cookies, cheese and crackers, pop, bottled water, juice, hot chocolate, sloppy Joes, breads and dips, leftovers, fruit baskets, candy, popcorn, pretzels, desserts, and seasonal foods.

- Thank everyone in person and in writing. And don't forget to continue thanking your "regular" volunteers. Don't ever take them for granted.

- Teach young adults new skills, for example, a new computer program. Provide leadership training, perhaps asking if they would consider doing some public speaking. Inviting them to go beyond their comfort zone can be a worthwhile challenge. Often the "teaching" can be done by another volunteer.

- Give people the option of taking a different leadership role if they are ready to move on to something else. Never assume that the person who has had a particular job for the past two years wants to stay in that job. Ask. Don't presume.

- Evaluate periodically. Who is working well? Who is ready for more responsibility? Are we making progress fast enough? What else could volunteers do to assist the ministry? Are we ready for new volunteers?

- Keep inviting younger faces. There is a great deal to be said for veterans training newcomers. There is also a great deal to be learned from the wisdom of the youngest young adults. To keep a good balance, you need to keep inviting twenties people. You can either pair them with experienced thirties people, or form a committee of just twenties people. As long as they can connect with someone more experienced to answer their questions, they will get the job done. Your goal should be a healthy mix of ages, talent levels, backgrounds, and lifestyles of young adult women and men.

Volunteers beyond the Office

Many young adults are highly altruistic. They are seeking ways to do more than work and work out. Many have had significant volunteer and service experiences during their college years and are looking for more opportunities to serve. In response, we created a program called Volunteers-in-Action, which links agencies in the Chicago area in need of volunteers with the young adults who contact us. The coordinator of this program, Michelle Doyle, is a volunteer herself. She comes into the office once a week to check messages, connect with agencies, return phone

Photo by Dan Hecker

Who says joining in the spring clean-up of the local shelter can't be a blast!

calls, distribute information, and update the Volunteers-in-Action list of opportunities to volunteer.

Michelle is a certified public accountant by profession. This volunteer work allows her to activate gifts she cannot use in her full-time job. After observing her work on several young adult projects, we personally invited Michelle to assume full responsibility for the Volunteers-in-Action program.*

Volunteers-in-Action is a referral program to help young adults who want to share their time and talent to find organizations in need of their help. The program began with a list of six organizations and has grown to include more than eighty.

Here are some options for volunteer programs:

Model 1: Work. Provide a referral network between volunteers and places where their help is needed. This model works best on the diocesan level, where people can be directed to places within their own communities. Volunteers-in-Action is this type of referral network.

Model 2: Work and Connect. Provide opportunities for people to come together for the purpose of volunteering. Young adults interested in achieving a common goal meet at a particular time and place and work together as a group. This model works well on the regional level.

---

*Much of the information below was presented by Michelle at a gathering we hosted for diocesan and parish leaders interested in dealing more effectively with their young adults. We thank Michelle for dedicated service and for the wisdom presented here.

Model 3: Work, Connect, and Go Deeper. Like model 2 above, this model brings young adults together to work, but then adds an element of theological reflection. People are called together to discuss their volunteer experience, what they saw and what they learned from their work along with any other insights and feelings about it. This model is ideal for the parish setting, because distance is not so much of an issue.

Before you begin any volunteer or social outreach program, ask, "What is the goal?" Goals might include: to give people options for volunteering, to build community, to enable participants to grow deeper spiritually, or to do all three. A parish young adult group can do all three. By volunteering, people will naturally build community with one another. Sharing their gifts gives them a sense of church.

Next, depending upon your goal, decide how many organizations you want to contact. Sometimes, one or two organizations is plenty, especially if you are visiting them on a frequent basis. If you want to give people a variety of options, you will want to consider more.

After you have decided how many organizations to contact, there is some specific information to be obtained:

- Who is the contact person? (Many organizations have a volunteer coordinator on staff.)
- What specific tasks does the organization need done?
- How often?
- What specific skills are required?
- What population group does this organization serve?
- What is the time requirement? (daily, weekly, monthly)
- Is any training necessary?

For our Volunteers-in-Action referral network, Michelle obtained the following information about each organization: agency name, task, time commitment, contact person, and phone number. The information is published regularly in our newsletter and is always available on our website. With this information, young adults can call the agency directly. However, if they have questions or concerns, they can call Michelle. She maintains a file for each organization, complete with brochures and additional facts.

Michelle often sends out flyers of several potential agencies to help young adults decide whom to call.

Although there is no lack of good will among young adults, many obstacles get in the way of volunteering, such as travel schedules for their jobs, long hours at work, and changes in work schedules. Michelle advises young adults who are serious about volunteering that there are options. One is to find a back-up. Michelle explained, "One woman I know was volunteering at a hospital and could not commit to every Tuesday evening. She found a friend, and between the two of them, they could cover every Tuesday night. She always had someone in place to cover for her on days she worked late, when she was sick, and when she went on vacation."

Another option is to coordinate with a few other friends. We have had volunteers visit the Metropolitan Correctional Center in Chicago. They were looking for people to help with a Sunday prayer service. Visiting a prison can be intimidating. We organized a group of thirty people to go one weekend, and it was fine. "People want to volunteer," Michelle said, "but it's intimidating to do something for the first time, and it's intimidating to do it alone. Organize events people can do with others. They may take the ball and run with it eventually, but in the beginning, if you set people up to work in groups, you tend to get a better response."

Another obstacle is that sometimes people say, "No, I don't have the skills," to tutor, for example. Given a well-run program where other adults are present, it is not usually a matter of having the right skills. It is more about establishing a relationship with a child than working on a specific skill. Most of the time the skills needed by the volunteers are extremely basic. If you don't know something, it can be a good opportunity to teach the child problem-solving skills: ask someone else, read the textbook further, or consult an encyclopedia.

Old St. Patrick's Church in Chicago has established "The Community Outreach Group." There people can choose where they want to volunteer from among several opportunities, for example: visit children in the hospital, provide meals at the shelter, tutor children, teach in an adult literacy program. Members meet on the steps of the church or in the parish reception area and car pool to their site. People know they can come as often as they are available. No one is tied down, and each organization has a crew of workers weekly. There is room for everyone, and more people can connect.

Here are some additional suggestions, strategies, and events to try:

- *Plan around the seasons of the year.* Particularly during Lent and Advent, people want to find a way to give. Help them to do so. Every Christmas, the Young Adult Ministry Office hosts a comedy night to benefit the work of Catholic Charities. They need twenty thousand gifts, and we have young adults eager for a night out. So the first Friday in December, we host "Give a Gift, Get a Giggle" in a parish hall. We serve pizza (which has been purchased at a discount) and beverages and then enjoy a show by members of a local comedy club. The admission price is $15, plus a toy for the toy drive (or $25 without a toy). Every year the number of participants grows. The comedy is good, clean fun, and after the show people can stay and enjoy one another. About forty volunteers help with decorations, registration, serving pizza and beverages, packing toys, and cleaning up. It is a night packed with fun, done in a true spirit of giving.

- *Conduct a volunteers' retreat.* Something happens to the people who volunteer. Invite them to come together and share their experiences, either positive or negative. Invite a few people to write out an experience that can be shared in your newsletter.

- *Follow up with the volunteers.* Ask, "How was your experience? Are you still volunteering? How is it going? Any suggestions for others who call to volunteer?" Young adults will not hesitate to let you know what worked and what did not. If they had a bad experience, you may have the opportunity to direct them into another situation.

- *Host a volunteer fair.* We host a volunteer fair once a year, where organizations come after the young adult Mass and share information about their work. Do it in February, when people are looking for things to do, and link it with an event where people are already gathering.

- If you are working on the diocesan level, *broker opportunities to local parishes.* If you create a list of opportunities like our Volunteers-in-Action list, parish and regional young adult groups can use it as well.

Make it as easy as possible for people to volunteer—both within your office and beyond it. Encourage them. Where you see talent, nurture it, develop it, and watch it grow. Find people's gifts and call them forward. When we support one another's gifts, we are in communion with one another. That is church at its best: the Body of Christ.

Conclusion

Our Preferential Option

In the very first sentence of chapter 1, we mentioned that the backbone of Catholic parish life not too many years ago was people twenty-five to forty-five years old, married or single. We believe that an effective ministry to young adults in our dioceses and throughout all of our parishes and Catholic organizations can make that happen again. We do not wish to be aging congregations but intergenerational communities.

In many areas of Catholic life, young adult people are just not present. Social surveys and serious research are not needed to come to that conclusion. Just as often, when young adults are seen even in small numbers, the comment can be heard, "My, look at the young people here today!"

However, social surveys and serious research have revealed a very important point about contemporary Catholic life. People are not leaving the Catholic Church, but in fact continue to affiliate at about the same rate people did thirty years ago.

The goal of young adult ministry and, for that matter, all Catholic Church ministry is a simple one: to invite affiliative Catholics into fuller practice and participation in the Catholic Church, allowing their gifts, talents, skills, and faith to contribute, through our church, to the building of a better world, God's kingdom on earth.

What would our church look like if its parishes, agencies, and organizations made a commitment to regenerate all aspects of church life with the presence of young adults in their twenties and thirties?

What would it be like if open positions for catechists, liturgical ministers, ministers of care, members of parish governance, and so forth, were filled primarily with young adult people?

What would Catholic life of our dioceses look like if Catholic agencies—Family Life, Divorce Ministry, Widows and Widowers, Evangeliza-

174

tion, Adult Catechesis, Parish Governance, Ethnic Ministries, Divine Worship, Peace and Justice, Lay Ministry Training, Vocations, the Respect Life Office, Men's Ministries, the Council of Catholic Women, the Bishop's Advisory Board, Catholic Charities—proactively added to their members, their ministerial outreach, their committees, and their governing boards Catholics between the ages of twenty and forty?

What would be the result if Catholic organizations were willing and able to regenerate their membership and their activities with the presence, talent, ideas, and energy of young adults?

The answer to all four questions is the same. *Our church would have life in abundance!*

Young adult ministry as described in this book is not the sole responsibility of a diocesan Young Adult Ministry Office, a parish young adult committee, a staff person in the age group, or the participants of a young adult group. A ministry to young adults is the responsibility of the whole church—from the bishop to all the baptized. All are members of the Catholic Church, whether they are affiliative or faithfully practicing, registered in the local parish or just living in the area, active in parish ministries and Catholic organizational life or just ordinary "pew Catholics."

Not too many years ago, sincere Catholic leaders began calling for a preferential option for the poor. In this twenty-first century, what would our church be like if we created and acted upon a preferential option for our own young adults? We might discover what Jesus proclaimed: "I have come that you may have life, and life in abundance."

Appendix A

Why Young Adult Catholics Go to Church and Why They Do Not

Fr. Terry Keehan

A 1998 study of young adult Catholics at six churches across the United States revealed that their principal reason for attending church is its sense of community while their chief reason for not attending is being too busy.

These were the findings of a six-month sabbatical during which I stayed for two to three weeks at each of six parishes, interviewing young adults and inquiring about their young adult programs. Each of the six has a strong reputation for welcoming young adults, that is, people between the ages of twenty and forty. The parishes and their youth ministers are:

Church of the Presentation, Upper Saddle River, New Jersey

Old St. Joseph's, Philadelphia

Church of the Annunciation, Altamonte Springs, Florida

Basilica of St. Mary, Minneapolis

St. Monica, Santa Monica, California

Old St. Patrick's, Chicago

I asked each pastor to identify ten young adults active in his church and then asked each of those ten to interview at least ten peers who do not go to church. These interviews were based on a questionnaire developed by sociologists Mary Ellen Konieczny-Chwedyck and Bill McCreedy. I believed peers interviewing each other would elicit the greatest candor. I collected the data from the questionnaires and interviewed the actively participating young adults.

At each of the six parishes, I held open meetings and discussions, during which I listened to what young adults had to say regarding their participation in church. In addition to the six parishes listed above, I also interviewed young adults in Dubuque, Iowa; Omaha, Nebraska; Cincinnati, Ohio; Ada, Ohio; and Long Island, New York, among other places. In total, I collected more than 500 questionnaires from those who do not go to church and conducted interviews with more than 450 young adults who go to church.

Why Catholic Young Adults Don't Go to Church

The five principal reasons given by Catholic young adults for not attending church are these:

1. I'm too busy to go to church: **28 percent.**

2. I disagree with one or several of the church's teachings: **23 percent.**

   Birth control: 61.5 percent (of the 23 percent)

   Women's equality/ ban on priesthood: 34.6 percent (of the 23 percent)

   Celibate priesthood: 19.2 percent (of the 23 percent)

3. I have negative childhood and adolescent memories of being forced to attend church, and when I was no longer forced to go to church I stopped, got out of the habit, or no longer feel obligated: **14.5 percent.**

4. I'm too lazy to go to church: **13.5 percent.**

5. There's too much ritual in the Catholic Church, or I don't like ritual: **13.5 percent.**

The fact that so many indicate that a busy schedule prevents them from going to church says something about American culture at the dawn of the twenty-first century. People fill their days and nights with much activity. While many commented that being too busy is merely an excuse, others remarked that young adults would find time if the experience of church were more spiritually nourishing, uplifting, or contemporary.

Disagreement with church teaching has been consistent through the years, so the second most common response for not attending church should come as no surprise. So too, the third most common answer is consistent with comments made for years: many young adults were forced to go to church by very loyal churchgoing parents. But children are forced to go to school and participate in other activities as well. It leads one to consider whether some factor in our religious development might actually encourage rebellion. After all, every culture, religion, and young generation has demonstrated a similar pattern in which each adolescent generation seems to move away from religious structure, then returns to raise its own children within the structure. Worthy of note, however, is researcher Wade Clark-Roof's finding that Baby Boomers, as a generation, have not returned to religious structures at as high a rate as have previous generations.

Perhaps the response of "too much ritual" will evoke the most reflection. This study notes that 13.5 percent of young adults believe there is too much ritual in the Catholic Church. Yet many in this same generation run to the home of a deceased celebrity to place flowers and candles. Ritual is precious to all humans, providing powerful expression to non-verbal communication. The church has missed a huge opportunity with many young people by failing to provide proper teaching on the meanings origin, history, and purpose of our religious tradition. It is ironic that in an age when young people hunger for ritual, the Catholic Church, with its rich tradition of ritual, somehow misses out.

Why Catholic Young Adults Go to Church

The five principal reasons given by churchgoing young adult Catholics for attending church are the following:

1. I've had positive experiences of community (I feel supported, connected, or encouraged; I'm an active participant; I feel a sense of belonging at church; I share faith, values, camaraderie, fellowship with others like me): **38 percent.**

2. Going to church helps me reflect (it gives me a perspective or focus; it helps clarify values, meaning, purpose in life; it offers a relevant message; it helps me cope; it gives me strength): **17.5 percent.**

3. I pray and feel close to God (it helps me maintain a relationship with God; I seek a weekly renewal of my relationship with God; I experience God's love): **17 percent.**

4. I give thanks to God at church (I go to experience the Eucharist; the real presence of Jesus in Eucharist/communion): **14 percent.**

5. The church has helped me grow spiritually (I want to grow, develop more; it addresses the void; it feeds my hunger for spiritual things): **10 percent.**

In many ways the answer that community encourages church participation is not new. The motivation of wanting to be a part of a gathering is classically Christian. Christians participate in an apostolic church founded by Jesus on the premise that connecting with God is not just a personal experience. The relationship with God is both public and private in nature.

The question posed was, "Why do you go to church?" not, "Why do you go to Mass." Young adults do not limit the experience of church to what happens on Sunday. They participate in other spiritual activities such as retreats, discussion groups, and Scripture groups as well as social activities and meaningful service projects. They are quick to use words like "supported," "connected," "participate," "active," "belonging," and "camaraderie" in describing their positive experiences of church.

Nearly 18 percent say church helps to give them perspective or to clarify meaning in life by inviting reflection. Relevant messages heard in homilies, in discussion groups, or on retreats help people to apply the Gospel to their lived experience. Young adults clearly place a high priority on this expectation of parish, Mass, and other church programs.

The third motivating factor is the classic, "I go to church to pray." Seeking a weekly renewal of one's relationship with God through participation in the worship experience of the community has nourished Christians. In fact, the instinct to gather with others in prayer is as old as humanity itself.

The fourth reason given, the real presence of Jesus in the Eucharist, was cited by only 14 percent of young adult respondents as a motivation for participation in church. This is another example of a great treasure of the Roman Catholic tradition that addresses many young adults' basic needs, but has been improperly explained. Eucharist means to give thanks.

Perhaps these precious rituals have been institutionalized and legalized to such a degree that they have slipped far from their original meaning.

The fifth reason is that church helps young adults to grow and develop spiritually. This response is related to the other four, but enough people articulated it in such similar fashion that it merited its own category. Many mentioned their spiritual hunger here, which is both honest and encouraging. Young adults are seekers. They are actively learning and using technology wisely to assist in their pursuits; it is healthy that young adults are seeking things spiritual as well.

Concluding Reflections

Between high school and their mid-thirties, many Baby Boomers asked their parents why it is important to go to church. Some parents were insulted by the question. It was interpreted as disrespectful to one of their most sacred institutions—the church. They never asked this question themselves because they were so loyal. They were (and still are) joiners and participators. Most parents never really answered the question. Perhaps the catechism that they studied did not permit them to question or analyze religion and faith the way younger people do. Consequently, many Baby Boomers have never received a satisfactory answer to the question or had a decent adult experience of church that has nourished them. They have never seen the church as a place to seek support or help, or even as a place to help make sense of the struggles of life.

Baby Boomers who attend church, on the other hand, know exactly why they go. They have claimed church in a very real way for themselves. Not as many still attend because it is the religion of their parents; they have questioned, left, and returned to the church on their own terms for reasons they clearly articulate.

Generation Xers have grown up with little of the Catholic culture of their predecessors, the Baby Boomers. While Boomers were raised in the language and structure of the church of the 1950s and 1960s, Generation Xers experienced less of the structures and rules and so had less to rebel against or question. They now seek structure to help make sense of their very chaotic world. These young people seem more open to the wisdom, tradition, stability, and peace that the church offers. They also appear to be more open to the moral guidance that the church offers than Baby Boomers are. Like their predecessors they are very willing to engage in service projects and other activities that they perceive to be significant.

Both Baby Boomers and Generation Xers have lived their entire lives in a consumer-oriented atmosphere. Much more so than their parents, they will shop for an experience of church that nourishes them.

Appendix B

A Daily Lenten Journey

Below is a series of reflections we posted on our website every day during Lent. Our goal was to feed the spiritual hunger of young adults, while helping them to experience Lent more fully. Also, we wanted to provide young adults with good reasons to keep visiting the website. We kept the information on "How to take this daily journey" along the right column of the screen, and put the opening prayer in the left column, followed by the meditation of the day and the closing prayer. Previous days' meditations were placed below the closing prayer. Feel free to adapt the website design to your own purposes.

These meditations were written by the authors and by Elise Ainsworth, a young adult intern who was working with us at the time. Her insights and faith were a marvelous addition.

A Daily Prayer Journey for Lent 2000, Cycle B

How to take this daily journey:

1. Begin with the Sign of the Cross.

2. Slowly (and out loud if possible) pray the opening prayer.

3. Read the Scripture passage . . . one, two, or three times.

4. Be still for at least a minute, and let the reading run through your mind.

5. Ponder the reflection and/or answer the question.

6. Add any personal prayers or intentions.

7. Pray the closing prayer.

8. End with the Sign of the Cross.

Opening Prayer:

God of my life, help me be still these next few minutes that I may open my mind, heart, and spirit to your presence. May your Word and your encouragement inspire me during this Lenten time of reflection and prayer. I pray to you through Christ, our Lord. Amen.

Closing Prayer:

Loving, ever-gracious God, stay close to me as I journey through this season of Lent. Lead me in your ways. May the actions of my life, each and every day, reveal your presence, love, kindness, and justice to all whom I meet. I pray through Christ, our Lord. Amen.

Ash Wednesday

Scripture: *We implore you, in Christ's name: be reconciled to God!* (2 Cor. 5:20)

For further meditation, the **lectionary readings** for the day are: Joel 2:12–18; 2 Corinthians 5:20–6:2; Matthew 6:1–6, 16–18.

Reflection: What does it mean to be reconciled to God? Our task over these forty days is to grow more in likeness to Christ. What one thing must I do during this Lenten season to more resemble the Lord of my life?

Thursday, Week 1

Scripture: *Jesus said to them all, "If any want to become my followers, let them deny themselves and take up their cross daily and follow me."* (Luke 9:23)

Lectionary readings: Deuteronomy 30:15–20; Luke 9:22–25

Reflection: You pay a price for anything of value. In the life of Christ, there was no Easter without Good Friday. For Christ's followers, there is no fullness of life without some suffering and hardship. What is your cross right now? Can you see a way that by bearing your cross, others are more fully alive? Spend a few minutes thanking Jesus for walking with you in this situation and for giving you the strength to persevere.

Friday, Week 1

Scripture: *[Thus says the Lord:] "This is the fasting that I wish: releasing those bound unjustly, untying the thongs of the yoke; setting free the oppressed,* *breaking every yoke; sharing your bread with the hungry, sheltering the oppressed and the homeless; clothing the naked when you see them, and not turning your back on your own. Then your light shall break forth like the dawn."* (Isaiah 58:6–8)

Lectionary readings: Isaiah 58:1–9; Matthew 9:14–15

Reflection: We are clearly called to extend care and compassion to others. It is not enough to take care of "me." Who do you know who needs support, and what can you do to respond to the challenge of God found in the words of Isaiah? Remember, it is not always easy or comfortable to do God's will.

Saturday, Week 1

Scripture: *If you remove from your midst oppression, false accusation, and malicious speech; if you bestow your bread on the hungry and satisfy the afflicted; then light shall rise for you in the darkness, and the gloom shall become for you like midday; then the Lord will guide you always.* (Isaiah 58:9–11)

Lectionary readings: Isaiah 58:9–14; Luke 5:27–32

Reflection: Say good things about people. Maybe that's the Lord's suggestion—for us to remove malicious speech. Is there someone you can call and make feel good about being alive? That could be a wonderful way for "light to rise" for you (and for them) in the darkness.

Sunday, Week 2

Scripture: *The Spirit sent Jesus out toward the desert. He stayed in the wasteland forty days, put to the test there by Satan.* (Mark 1:12–13)

Lectionary readings: Genesis 9:8–15; 1 Peter 3:18–22; Mark 1:12–15

Reflection: In school, we are quizzed on how well we know a subject. Here's your quiz today: What does it mean to be a son or daughter of God? When is it hardest to believe that's who you are? What gets in the way of your true identity? Is there anything you want to do about that?

Monday, Week 2

Scripture: *You shall not bear hatred toward your brother or sister in your heart.* (Leviticus 19:17)

Lectionary readings: Leviticus 19:1–2, 11–18; Matthew 25:31–46

Reflection: It's hard not to hate sometimes. It's even more difficult not to hold a grudge, especially when you've been hurt badly. Is there someone against whom you are holding a grudge or bitter feelings? That person may never be your friend, but today, can you find a way to let go of some of the anger and pain? You might want to try giving it to God (offer it up). It won't be easy to let go and move on, but you will be a better person. You know that . . . and so does God.

Tuesday, Week 2

Scripture: *Thy kingdom come, Thy will be done. . . .* (Matthew 6:10)

Lectionary readings: Isaiah 55:10–11; Matthew 6:7–15

Reflection: We pray the Our Father every time we go to Mass. Pray it again now, slowly, reverently. Then, go back a second time. When you get to the line "Thy will be done" stop and name a situation where you want and need God's loving support and guidance. After you name it, add, "Thy will be done." Any others? After each, add, "Thy will be done." End with a prayer of thanksgiving that God is with us and understands our struggles and pain.

Wednesday, Week 2

Scripture: *"For at the preaching of Jonah they reformed, but you have a greater one than Jonah here."* (Luke 11:32)

Lectionary readings: Jonah 3:1–10; Luke 11:29–32

Reflection: The book of Jonah is satire—a wonderful story of just how hard it is for people to change their ways. A preacher that nobody knew caused everyone to change, including the king and the cattle. The point is a simple one: it's ever so hard to change just because someone says so. What are you holding on to that, if you let it go—even just a little—you would be a better person? Talk it over with God.

Thursday, Week 2

Scripture: *"Treat others the way you would have them treat you: this sums up the law and the prophets."* (Matthew 7:12)

Lectionary readings: Esther 12:14–16, 23–25; Matthew 7:7–12

Reflection: Make a list of the five ways you would like all people to treat you. Use that list as five strategic ways you can, should, and must treat others. How about asking the Lord today for the courage to do that?

Friday, Week 2

Scripture: *"If you bring your gift to the altar and there recall that your brother or sister has anything against you, leave your gift at the altar, go first to be reconciled to your brother or sister, then come and offer your gift."* (Matthew 5:23–24)

Lectionary readings: Ezekiel 18:21–28; Matthew 5:20–26

Reflection: Our faith is not about us and God solely or exclusively. Jesus reminds us today that our faith is all about God, us, and our neighbors. Our faith in God can only be as strong as our ability to live in communion with other people. Today, call to mind one or two people with whom you experience stress, pain, or alienation. Ask the Lord for wisdom and assistance to heal those relationships.

Saturday, Week 2

Scripture: *And today the Lord is making this agreement with you: you are to be God's own people, as God promised you; and provided you keep all God's commandments, God will then raise you high in praise and renown and glory above all other nations God has created. You will be a people sacred to the Lord, your God.* (Deuteronomy 26:18–19)

Lectionary readings: Deuteronomy 26:16–19; Matthew 5:43–48

Reflection: Do you believe that? You are sacred to the Lord, your God! All too often we let other people define who we really are. If our job is good, we are good. If we have lots of friends, we are good. If we are seen as successful, we are good. We are sacred to God when we are successful or struggling, alone or with others, at work, at home, on the running trail, at the gym, at our desks. We are sacred to God—today and every day. That's God's commitment to us. Why not take a few moments and let that sink in?

Sunday, Week 3

Scripture: *"This is my son, my beloved. Listen to Him."* (Mark 9:7)

Lectionary readings: Genesis 22:1–2, 9, 10–13, 15–18; Romans 8:31–34; Mark 9:2–10

Reflection: To really listen to someone can be hard work. We love to talk, and often we are preparing a response before someone else has even finished speaking. Many people are very good at quoting Scripture or telling others what Jesus said. Today, it is time to "listen to him." Why not just be still for a little while, and let some of the words of the Lord that you love and cherish speak to you in quiet?

Monday, Week 3

Scripture: *"Be compassionate as your God is compassionate. Do not judge, and you will not be judged. Do not condemn, and you will not be condemned. Forgive and you shall be forgiven."* (Luke 6:36–37)

Lectionary readings: Daniel 9:4–10; Luke 6:36–38

Reflection: Easier said than done! Our world today seems so quick to judge others, to shout words of condemnation, and ever so slow to forgive and forget. Many have said that we are becoming an intolerant society. It cannot be like that with us, God's people. To walk with Christ means that our behavior and language are filled with compassion and respect for others, even for those with whom we have major disagreements. "Be compassionate as your God is compassionate."

Tuesday, Week 3

Scripture: *"The greatest among you will be the one who serves the rest. All who exalt themselves will be humbled, and all who humble themselves will be exalted."* (Matthew 23:11–12)

Lectionary readings: Isaiah 1:10, 16–20; Matthew 23:1–12

Reflection: The social order of daily life says that greatness comes from power, fame, money, title, and influence. The spiritual order of life sees it another way. Greatness is all about service. And service for the Lord Jesus means that we must pour God's life into other people. That's the path to glory. And what is God's life that we pour into others by serving them? A deep respect for them, loving them for their humanity, forgiving them their mistakes, being honest in our dealings with them. We are made in God's image. Take a moment now and reflect on how you might be able to pour God's life into others this Lenten day.

Wednesday, Week 3

Scripture: *"Anyone among you who aspires to greatness must serve the rest, and whoever wants to rank first among you must serve the needs of all."* (Matthew 20:26–27)

Lectionary readings: Jeremiah 18:18–20; Matthew 20:17–28

Reflection: So much of Christ's message works the opposite of how we think it should work. It is in giving that we receive. It is in feeding others that we are fed. And in order to gain life in abundance, you have to give life away. Spend a few minutes considering some of the ways you give life to others. Give thanks for the people in your life who share their life and love with you.

Thursday, Week 3

Scripture: *Jesus said, "Once there was a rich man who dressed in purple and linen and feasted splendidly every day. At his gate lay a beggar named Lazarus...."* (Luke 16:19–20)

Lectionary readings: Jeremiah 17:5–10; Luke 16:19–31

Reflection: Do you ever wonder why some people seem to have so much while others seem to have so little? The story of Lazarus is about the way we respond to those less fortunate. One of the reasons we "give things up" during Lent is so that there will be more for others. Before this time tomorrow, how can you share some of your time, talent, or treasure with another?

Friday, Week 3

Scripture: *"I tell you, the kingdom of God will be taken away from you and given to a nation that will yield a rich harvest."* (Matthew 21:43)

Lectionary readings: Genesis 37:3–4, 12–13, 17–28; Matthew 21:33–43, 45–46

Reflection: There is a very wise strategy about life and business: presume little; explain lots. It fits the words of the Lord today. Faith can't ever be presumed or simply taken for granted. It is not a possession as much as it is an activity and way of life. It must always be acted upon. Today we are being asked to be faithful people—in action, prayer, and words. What faithful activity will give God's life to another person? Do it! For what do you need God's assistance? Pray for it. What about your faith is so special? Believe it!

Saturday, Week 3

Scripture: *Who is there like you, the God who removes guilt and pardons sins for the remnant of his inheritance? Who does not persist in anger forever, but delights rather in clemency, and will again have compassion on us, treading underfoot our guilt?* (Micah 7:18–19)

Lectionary readings: Micah 7:14–15, 18–20; Luke 15:1–3, 11–32

Reflection: Have you ever boasted about a friend to someone else? It is such a wonderful way to understand the meaning, power, and presence of a great relationship: putting it in words and sharing it. The prophet Micah is boasting about the wonders of God. Your turn. Boast to yourself or write down, as if in a letter to a friend, the meaning, impact, power, and presence of God in your life.

Sunday, Week 4

Scripture: *Remember to keep holy the Sabbath day. Six days you may labor and do all your work, but the seventh day is the Sabbath of the Lord, your God. On the seventh day, God rested. That is why the Lord has blessed the Sabbath day and made it holy.* (Exodus 20:8–11)

Lectionary readings: Exodus 20:1–17; 1 Corinthians 1:22–25; John 2:13–25

Reflection: Times have changed dramatically. Sunday (Sabbath) is far from a day of rest. It has become the busiest shopping day of the week! Yet the importance of Sabbath rest hasn't changed. We need a time that reminds us we are not our job or our routine. So what do you do on Sunday that you don't do any other day of the week? Name it. If you can't, then find something life-giving to do—at least once a week—that will remind you that you are a child of God. Start today.

Monday, Week 4

Scripture: *When Jesus had come to Nazareth, he said to the people in the synagogue, "Truly I tell you, no prophet is accepted in the prophet's hometown."* (Luke 4:24)

Lectionary readings: 2 Kings 5:1–15; Luke 4:24–30

Reflection: The older we get, the harder it is to change. People, especially family and friends, expect us to be and to act a certain way. And very often we try to "be like everybody else." However, there is a life within us— God's life. It calls us to live and act as a person who pours God's life and love into others. Can you name some moments when the expectations of family and friends held you back? Can you name something that God's life within might be calling you to do or be?

Tuesday, Week 4

Scripture: *Peter came up and asked Jesus, "Lord, when my brother wrongs me, how often must I forgive him? Seven times?" "No," Jesus replied, "not seven times; I say, seventy times seven times."* (Matthew 18:21–22)

Lectionary readings: Daniel 3:25, 34–43; Matthew 18:21–35

Reflection: To forgive someone who has wronged you is one of the most difficult things to do. After all, you have been wronged. Someone did something to you. Yet the call of faith is to be a forgiving person—always and forever. Not many people seem to be able to do that. Have a conversation with the Lord today and review with the Lord some of the situations in your life that are in need of forgiveness and healing. Ask the Lord for some wisdom on how that might be accomplished.

Wednesday, Week 4

Scripture: *Jesus said to his disciples, "Do not think that I have come to abolish the law and the prophets. I have come to fulfill them. . . . That is why whoever* *breaks the least significant of these commands and teaches others to do so shall be called least in the kingdom of God. Whoever fulfills and teaches these commands shall be great in the kingdom of God."* (Matthew 5:17, 19)

Lectionary readings: Deuteronomy 4:1, 5–9; Matthew 5:17–19

Reflection: Faith in God is not so much about following rules and conforming to laws as it is giving witness by example to God's presence in this world. That's what it means to fulfill and teach the commands of God. How do you see yourself, quietly yet publicly, giving witness to the presence and teaching of the law and the prophets? Conversely, when and where is it difficult to do so?

Thursday, Week 4

Scripture: *Thus says the Lord, "This is what I command my people: Listen to my voice, then I will be your God and you shall be my people. Walk in the ways I command you, so that you may prosper."* (Jeremiah 7:23)

Lectionary readings: Jeremiah 7:23–28; Luke 11:14–23

Reflection: How do we listen? Easy. Someone must first speak. Today try to listen to the Lord in a different kind of way. Just be still and silent. Do nothing. Think nothing. Say nothing. Simply close your eyes. Remove as many distractions as you can. Be still and totally quiet. Listen in silence. Sometimes in silence you can experience the presence of a loving God. Try it now for five minutes.

Friday, Week 4

Scripture: *[The Lord says:] "I will heal their disloyalty. I will love them freely. For my wrath is turned away from them."* (Hosea 14:4)

Lectionary readings: Hosea 14:2–10; Mark 12:28–34

Reflection: How comforting it is to know that the Lord loves us even when we fail, even when we feel unlovable. Here at the halfway point of Lent we may be disheartened by our struggles with our Lenten commitments, but Scripture reminds us of God's forgiveness and unconditional love for us.

Saturday, Week 4

Scripture: *Let us press on to know the Lord, whose appearing is as sure as the dawn. The Lord will come to us like the rain, like the spring rain that waters the earth.* (Hosea 6:3)

Lectionary readings: Hosea 6:1–6; Luke 18:9–14

Reflection: How comforting it is to know that our God comes to meet us. It doesn't always feel that way, though, especially at times when our prayers seem to go unheard. Trust that God is with you. Know that all prayer time is quality time—even when it doesn't produce what we hoped it would produce.

Sunday, Week 5

Scripture: *Early and often did the Lord, the God of their fathers, send his messengers to them, for he had compassion on his people and his dwelling place.* (2 Chronicles 36:15)

Lectionary readings: 2 Chronicles 36:14–17, 19–23; Ephesians 2:4–10; John 3:14–21

Reflection: God does not expect us to face the world alone. God is with us in spirit and through the people in our lives. Think about the messengers God has sent to you with a friendly smile, a reassuring hug, or a word of encouragement.

Monday, Week 5

Scripture: *[The Lord says:] "Lo, I am about to create new heavens and a new earth; the things of the past shall not be remembered."* (Isaiah 65:17)

Lectionary readings: Isaiah 65:17–21; John 4:43–54

Reflection: There is a great Christian song called "The Sea of Forgetfulness." It raises the question: God forgives and forgets our sins; why can't we? We are called to life in abundance. What do you need to cast into "the sea of forgetfulness" to be free? What is God creating anew in you?

Tuesday, Week 5

Scripture: *There is a place with the Hebrew name Bethesda . . . crowded with sick people lying there, blind, lame or disabled [waiting for the movement of the* *water]. There was a man who had been sick for thirty-eight years....* (John 5:2–5)

Lectionary readings: Ezekiel 47:1–9, 12; John 5:1–3, 5–16

Reflection: Some versions of the Bible include an additional verse in today's Gospel reading: "For [from time to time] an angel of the Lord used to come down into the pool; and the water was stirred up, so the first one to get in was healed of their sickness." The sick man had been waiting for someone to throw him into the pool, since he could not get in himself. When Jesus saw him, he healed him on the spot. Is there an area in your life where you await healing? Perhaps Jesus is the friend to turn to in your need.

Wednesday, Week 5

Scripture: *Thus says the Lord...* "*Along the ways they shall find pasture, on every bare height shall their pastures be. They shall not hunger and thirst, nor shall the scorching wind or sun strike them.*" (Isaiah 49:8–10)

Lectionary readings: Isaiah 49:8–15; John 5:17–30

Reflection: This passage from Isaiah reminds us that God has pity on God's children. At times we may feel imprisoned, but God helps us to free ourselves. Where have you seen the care and protection of the Lord in your life?

Thursday, Week 5

Scripture: *Jesus said to the Jews, ...* "*These very works which I perform testify on my behalf that the Father has sent me.*" (John 5:36)

Lectionary readings: Exodus 32:7–14; John 5:31–47

Reflection: What are the works of your life that testify on your behalf that the Father/Creator has sent you?

Friday, Week 5

Scripture: *[Jesus said:]* "*I was sent by the one who has the right to send, and him you do not know. I know him because it is from him I come. He sent me.*" (John 7:28–29)

Lectionary readings: Wisdom 2:1, 12–22; John 7:1–2, 10, 25–30

Reflection: We have secrets going on in both Scripture readings today. In this Gospel, the implied questions are: how can we know God, and how do we know what is from God? For us, the way to the Father/Creator is through the Son. How has your relationship with Jesus revealed God to you?

Saturday, Week 5

Scripture: *Some of the crowd wanted to apprehend Jesus, . . . but Nicodemus spoke up to say, "Since when does our law condemn any man without first hearing him and knowing the facts?"* (John 7:44, 50–51)

Lectionary readings: Jeremiah 11:18–20; John 7:40–53

Reflection: Have you ever felt condemned before you were given a chance to explain the facts? Have you ever jumped to conclusions about another without knowing the facts? Let's work on following Nicodemus's advice to listen attentively before acting.

Sunday, Week 6

Scripture: *"Unless the grain of wheat falls to the earth and dies, it remains just a grain of wheat. But if it dies, it produces much fruit."* (John 12:24)

Lectionary readings: Jeremiah 31:31–34; Hebrews 5:7–9; John 12:20–33

Reflection: The Christian story is constantly flowing from life to death then to new life. Is there a particular area in your life or the life of someone near to you where the grain of wheat is dying or needs to die before producing good fruit? Jesus never promised to take the pain of death away, but he did promise to walk with us through it. Trust that resurrection is near.

Monday, Week 6

Scripture: *[Jesus said to them:] "Let the one among you who has no sin be the first to cast a stone at her."* (John 8:7)

Lectionary readings: Daniel 13:1–9, 15–17, 19–30, 33–62; John 8:1–11

Reflection: Often it is hard for us to remember that it is not for us to judge others. Jesus reminds us to be more critical of our own ways and more forgiving of others. Today try to stop yourself from judging and simply accept others as they are.

Tuesday, Week 6

Scripture: *Jesus said, "The one who sent me is with me; he has not left me alone, for I always do what is pleasing to him."* (John 8:29)

Lectionary readings: Numbers 21:4–9; John 8:21–30

Reflection: Do you feel sent by God as gift to the world? You should. You are God's beloved one, chosen and sent to be a light to the world. May our prayer today be: "The one who sent me is with me; God has not left me alone, and I will do what is pleasing to God."

Wednesday, Week 6

Scripture: *[Jesus said:] "If you live according to my teaching, you are truly my disciples; then you will know the truth, and the truth will set you free."* (John 8:31–32)

Lectionary readings: Daniel 3:14–20, 91–92, 95; John 8:31–42

Reflection: At first our reaction to Jesus' statement might be similar to that of the people he was speaking to: we are free. Jesus tells us that whether we realize it or not we are enslaved by the sin in our lives. Maybe we are obliged to support our bad habits or perhaps we are not honest with ourselves about the effects of our actions on others and ourselves. Let us strive to be truthful in word and deed.

Thursday, Week 6

Scripture: *"The one who gives me glory is the very one you claim for your God, even though you do not know him. But I know him. I know him well and I keep his word."* (John 8:54–55)

Lectionary readings: Genesis 17:3–9; John 8:51–59

Reflection: What a joy it would be to proclaim in all honesty, "I know God well, and I keep God's word!" Our Lenten journey is a piece of our spiritual journey, where we strive "to know God well." God longs to be intimately in relationship with us. Let's pray for the grace to see and experience God's presence deeply in our lives.

Friday, Week 6

Scripture: *The Lord is with me, like a mighty champion; my persecutors will stumble. They will not triumph.* (Jeremiah 20:11)

Lectionary readings: Jeremiah 20:10–13; John 10:31–42

Reflection: How comforting it is to know that in the midst of all our struggles, God dwells. Call upon God to be a source of healing and support for anyone you know (including yourself) who is in the midst of a difficult time. Trust that God is with you.

Saturday, Week 6

Scripture: *Thus says the Lord God: "I will take the people of Israel from the nations among which they have gone, and will gather them from every quarter, and bring them to their own land."* (Ezekiel 37:21)

Lectionary readings: Ezekiel 37:21–28; John 11:45–57

Reflection: The Lord wants us to be one with one another and with God. God wishes us to be united in peace. How can you extend peace in your life?

Palm or Passion Sunday

Scripture: *"My God, my God, why have you forsaken me?"* (Mark 15:34)

Lectionary readings: Isaiah 50:4–7; Philippians 2:6–11; Mark 14:1–15:47

Reflection: Often this verse is used to help us believe in Jesus' humanity and know the depth of his suffering. He really did know pain and despair. When we are troubled, we can be comforted in turning to Jesus for empathy and companionship.

Monday, Holy Week

Scripture: *[God says of God's servant:] "A bruised reed he will not break, and a smoldering wick he will not quench; he will faithfully bring forth justice. He will not grow faint or be crushed until he establishes justice on the earth."* (Isaiah 42:3–4)

Lectionary readings: Isaiah 42:1–7; John 12:1–11

Reflection: This is what it means to be a follower or servant of God: Every day we must strive for justice in this world. If individually we can make our thoughts and actions just, then maybe our families and friends, homes and workplaces will be affected, and, like ripples in a pond, we will have an impact that we cannot imagine.

Tuesday, Holy Week

Scripture: *Simon Peter said to Jesus, "Lord, where are you going?" He answered, "Where I am going, you cannot follow me now; but you will follow afterward." Peter said to him, "Lord, why can I not follow you now? I will lay down my life for you." Jesus answered, "Will you lay down your life for me? Very truly, I tell you, before the cock crows, you will have denied me three times."* (John 13:36–38)

Lectionary readings: Isaiah 49:1–6; John 13:21–33, 36–38

Reflection: Actions speak louder than words. That certainly was true for Peter and most assuredly is true for us. During this Holy Week, let us reflect on the faithfulness of Jesus to us and to the God who gave him life. In Christ, actions speak no louder than his words. His actions and his words are identical.

Wednesday, Holy Week

Scripture: *When it was evening, he took his place with the twelve; and while they were eating, he said, "Truly I tell you, one of you will betray me." Then Judas spoke, "Surely it is not I, Rabbi?" He replied, "You have said so."* (Matthew 26:20–21, 25)

Lectionary readings: Isaiah 50:4–9; Matthew 26:14–25

Reflection: To betray a friend is such a terrible thing. That is obvious in the story of Judas and Jesus. Reflect on those you love and those you call friends. Have you ever spread gossip about any of them? What caused you to say unkind things? How might you have brought hurt into their lives? Betrayal takes many forms. If you have betrayed friends, ask God for forgiveness. Thank God for the gift of such wonderful people in your life.

Holy Thursday

Scripture: *"For I received from the Lord what I also handed on to you, that the Lord Jesus, on the night when he was betrayed, took a loaf of bread. When he had given thanks, he broke it and said, 'This is my body that is for you. Do this in remembrance of me.'"* (1 Corinthians 11:23–24)

Lectionary readings: Exodus 12:1–8, 11–14; 1 Corinthians 11:23–26; John 13:1–15

Reflection: How do you remember Jesus? How would you tell someone about him? Better still, what actions in your life tell the story of Jesus to others?

Good Friday

Scripture: *When they came to Jesus and saw that he was already dead, they did not break his legs. Instead, one of the soldiers pierced his side with a spear, and at once blood and water flowed out.* (John 19:33–34)

Lectionary readings: Isaiah 52:13–53:12; Hebrews 4:14–16; 5:7–9; John 18:1–19:42

Reflection: The entire mission of Jesus was to give life to the world. Even the act of dying was life-giving. The story about blood and water flowing from his side is a symbol of life. At our birth, blood and water preceded us into the world. The death of Jesus seen here is the continuance of his life being poured out to us all. Jesus, remember me when you come into your kingdom.

Holy Saturday

Scripture: *Lord, send out your Spirit, and renew the face of the earth.* (Psalm 104:30)

Lectionary readings: The following readings are proclaimed at the Easter Vigil service Saturday evening: Genesis 1:1–2:2; Genesis 22:1–18; Exodus 14:15–15:1; Isaiah 54:5–14; Isaiah 55:1–11; Baruch 3:9–15, 32–4:4; Ezekiel 36:16–28; Romans 6:3–11; Mark 16:1–8.

Reflection: It's Holy Saturday. We commemorate the day Jesus was in the tomb, and we use this day to look for life and the Lord of Life. And so, we pray: Lord, send out your Spirit. May your Spirit prompt us to bring your life to others, especially those who struggle to survive in mind or body. May the actions of our lives hint at what we celebrate with the resurrection of Easter Sunday: that God's life is stronger than death.

Easter Sunday

Scripture: *"They have taken the Lord out of the tomb, and we do not know where they have laid him." Then Peter and the other disciple set out and went toward the tomb. The two were running together, but the other disciple outran Peter and reached the tomb first.* (John 20:2–4)

Lectionary readings: Acts of the Apostles 10:34, 37–43; Colossians 3:1–4 or 1 Corinthians 5:6–8; John 20:1–9

Reflection: Love always outruns fear. Peter was in no hurry to encounter Jesus. At the last encounter, he denied knowing him. The other disciple was filled with love. Love is in a hurry to transform the world. It's Easter. The love of Jesus cannot be contained in a tomb. God's love for you knows no boundaries either. Let go. Let the love of the Risen Christ fill your spirit. Happy Easter!

Appendix C

The Database

One of the tenets of the Young Adult Ministry Office is to maintain connections. An effective tool for doing so is our Microsoft Access database, which we use to track activity and event participation. This relational database, containing thirty-two tables and twenty-one fields, stores an individual's demographic information as well as data on that person's participation.

The main screen of the database allows us to search by last name, first name, address, city, or individual ID. We can search on one or all of the fields. This is helpful when searching for individuals who have identical last names. A sample of the screen is shown below.

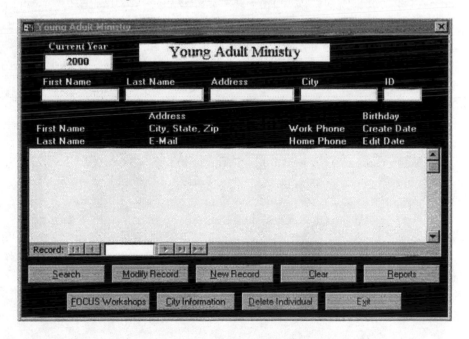

A sampling of the programs we track is shown on the database screen below.

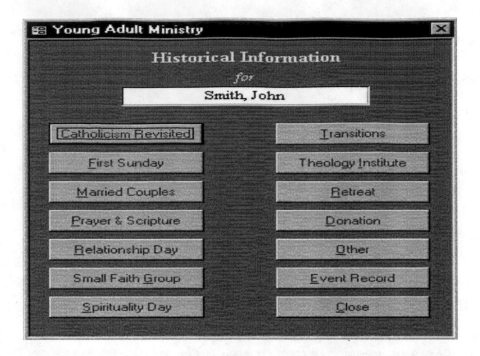

The database tracks all aspects of the FOCUS conference that is held every year. It allows us to keep track of everything from the finances of the conference to information on who registered for what workshops. We know how much money is spent on registration, lunches, and dinners. We are easily able to identify who volunteered at the conference or made an extra donation. Keeping track of this type of information is very useful in planning for future conferences. It helps us determine what workshops should be expanded and what workshops should be eliminated. Most importantly, it assists our office in reaching out to young adults. The data entry screen of our FOCUS conference is similar to our registration form.

Our database also helps us to learn about people's interests and activities. We are able to identify people who would be interested in future activities. Our database has been modified and used by the Young Adult Group at Holy Name Cathedral, the Crossroads Center at Old St. Patrick's

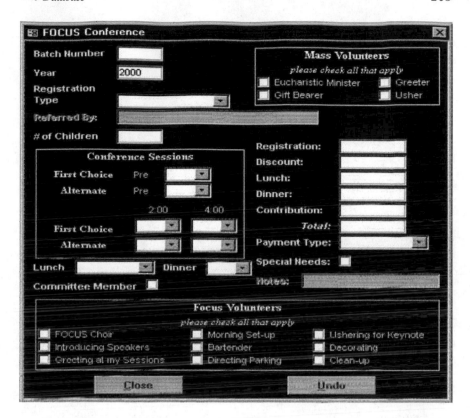

Church, and the First Friday Club of Chicago. If you would like information on creating your own database or would like a copy of the shell of our database, please contact David Barsotti at 312-466-9473.

Appendix D

Creating and Maintaining
a Dialogue Group

What I really would enjoy is gathering with people my age occasionally for some good conversation.

Though it is expressed in a variety of ways, there is a common need among many young adults for conversation about significant issues of daily life, contemporary society, morality and ethics, and religious and personal values. Yet, such a commonly expressed need seems to be one of the hardest to fill.

It's hard to find people who are interested. When you do, they seem really reluctant to join in a group.

I'd like to get something started, but I don't want to be the leader.

I don't have the background to keep up with people in a serious discussion on religion.

Those groups are really a disguise. They are not groups. They are either therapy for somebody or heavy church groups telling me what I have to believe and what I must do. So much for dialogue.

Despite such misgivings, people still want to find a successful "dialogue group," and the quest continues.

I have a real hunger to learn more and to be more. Some of the best things you learn don't come from a classroom.

I am more than my job.

I'm not looking for more friends. I am blessed with many! I am looking for insights into life I can't always get from friends.

I'm looking for knowledge and insights that aren't so much found in books as much as they are lived out in life.

I'm just curious about why people believe and what people believe.

A young adult dialogue group is a gathering of six to eight people for the purpose of sharing ideas and insights, for example, about issues of human experience, personal values, religious beliefs, or current affairs.

There is no one way for a young adult dialogue group to be effective. Groups can be totally different in their approach and style. There are only two common denominators for all young adult dialogue groups: age and dialogue. After that, variety is the cornerstone. Some groups are made up exclusively of single professionals, while others are married couples with small children. Some groups thrive on a blend of single and married people with various backgrounds and jobs. One group might be made up of people from the same community or parish, while another might represent people from various neighborhoods. Some groups will be overtly religious (Bible study, faith sharing), while others might have a much broader scope—focusing on current events or social issues not exclusively spiritual in nature. The possible structure and make-up of young adult dialogue groups are limitless. Moreover, the direction and focus of a group can change as people get to know one another, and other needs arise.

Here are some guidelines that should be helpful in designing, establishing, and maintaining an effective young adult dialogue group.

1. Determine as clearly as possible what you want.

Whether you want to begin a young adult dialogue group or are seeking to become a participant in one, you should clearly state what you are looking for, for example, a general discussion group, Bible study. Even ambiguity, clearly expressed, is proper: "I'm not really sure what I'm looking for, but I am willing to give it a try."

2. Beware of hidden agendas.

If a dialogue group is announced and the dialogue turns out to be a monologue of rules and moralisms, there was a hidden agenda. If people are expecting to speak from their own life experience and the leader is always asking, "What does Jesus say?" there is a hidden agenda. If it's designed for group participation and communication and only two people ever speak, that, too, is a hidden agenda.

3. Keep the importance of attendance in perspective.

Attendance is important, but not a matter of life or death. Members should not be expected to commit themselves to being present at every gathering. Make sure people have the freedom to come and go as they need to. If the group is important to participants, they will do their best to be present.

4. Personally invite people to participate.

If you are responsible for beginning a dialogue group, personally invite several other people to join the group. These should be people you know and trust and who reflect in themselves what you want the group to be. Sometimes it is difficult to put into words exactly what you want a dialogue group to be. It will take shape with the presence of certain people. They will help to incarnate your idea.

5. Start slowly.

Eagerness is essential. Overzealousness can be destructive. It might take weeks or months to find six to eight people to participate in a dialogue group. Proceed slowly and plan for lasting success. It might take several meetings for all the ingredients for success to be in place (the right people, a good comfort level, a workable process). Quality takes time.

6. Less leads to more.

Meeting even twice a month might be too often for some people's schedules. There is a natural tendency at the beginning of new ventures to overcommit. It is easier to decide, after a while, to meet more often than to decide, after a while, that the group is meeting too often.

7. Plan to meet for as many times as there are people in the group.

If the group is composed of seven people, then the seven should commit themselves, initially, to seven sessions. In this way, each person knows exactly how long the commitment will last. People also know how much time they have to learn about the people in the group.

8. Have each participant lead or suggest the theme and process for one session.

Everyone in the group will have expectations of what the group should be or should discuss. When people gather for the first time in a new group, each person present is often asked to state his or her hopes and expectations. If the group members each have the opportunity to set the agenda and establish the process for one session, their words of expectation or anticipation can be fleshed out in the group session for which they are responsible.

9. Vary the topics for dialogue.

It is possible to dialogue about politics, religion, current events, jobs, re-lationships, economics, personal goals, moral teachings, poetry, history, significant people, books, movies, beliefs, heroes, and so on. A young adult dialogue group should not lock itself too quickly into conversing in one area: "We will discuss a chapter of this book every week." People need to know what is important to others in the group and how the others view different topics. After several meetings, the group will discover interests they have in common.

10. Vary the process.

One session might be a straight, heady discussion of a serious topic: nuclear disarmament. Another could be a personal reflection on the impact our parents have on us. Still another group meeting might be spent discussing an article, an editorial, or a chapter of a book. The group might wish to dialogue about a passage of Scripture or comment on a prayer that is personally important. Another gathering might focus on heroes who have had an impact on members of the group or what it is about the future that causes people to wonder. One session could be devoted to sharing something that each person has written.

11. Give everyone a turn to respond to the topic before the floor is opened.

In any group there will be people who dominate the conversation and others who would rather just listen. In this group, everyone should be given an opportunity to share before people begin commenting on what others have said. This format insures that the introverts in the group are able to express their thoughts and share their experiences.

12. Set time limits for each session.

The leader or group consensus should determine the length of each meeting and stick to it. An hour and a half to two hours is adequate. Holding to that time frame is important. People then know exactly how much time they have committed and can make other plans. Sometimes the session length will seem too short. If so, the group might plan to return to the topic or process another time. On another occasion, an hour and a half might seem an eternity. In such a case, all present know exactly how much longer they must work to keep the discussion going.

13. Keep a record of recurring topics and themes.

Even with a different topic and a different process suggested or hosted by a different person at each meeting, certain themes, topics, ideas, questions, dilemmas, and issues are bound to recur. At least one person (and better two) should keep a log of these common issues. This should be done immediately after each session, when memories are most fresh. A catalog of recurring themes will help determine the future direction of the group after the initial number of meetings is completed. A record should be kept of the different processes, too. Which group process allowed for the most spontaneity? The best discussion? The least frustration? The best group interaction? Which was the least threatening and most helpful time for all?

14. Don't be afraid to start over.

After the initial commitment has expired, decisions need to be made. The group may choose to continue or to disband, and individuals may wish to leave the group. The person who had the original idea for the group might see the group taking on a character or moving in a direction different from what was hoped for or even decided upon. Change is inevitable and essential. If need be, let go. Staying too long with a situation that is no longer helpful or life-giving can lead to very strained relations. Start over. If belonging to a dialogue group is still important to you, then try again. Anything of value takes time, trial and error, and more time.

15. Talk through a medium.

Conversation is often aided by a medium such as an article or book. Written material gives you a starting place and supplies food for thought. It also can be inspirational and challenging. With each member of the group choosing material, the group can be introduced to a variety of authors, perspectives, and literary forms.

16. Use examples to help keep dialogue going.

Giving examples from lived experiences (your own or others) adds more insights, allows more possibilities, and leaves more room for further discussion than simply stating an opinion. Opinions tend to be more intellectual than practical and can lead to debate and arguments.

17. Don't be concerned about friendships.

Friendships may or may not develop. A young adult dialogue group is not expected to be anyone's primary social group. The atmosphere should be friendly, and if friendships arise, so much the better. Friendships are not an implied expectation. Participants' other relationships may take precedence and must always be respected. Remember, there are only two expectations: age and dialogue.

18. Respect confidentiality.

What is said in a dialogue group is best left there. Comments taken out of context can be harmful. Confidentiality is an ingredient that builds trust.

19. Consider splitting the group.

If, after the initial commitment, there are some clearly defined areas of conversation and interest, the group might wish to split around those issues. For example, one part of the group might wish to discuss issues in a more religious way, focusing on Scripture or the Catholic tradition, while another part of the group might thrive on a more open-ended approach. Both should be encouraged.

20. Call in "experts" only occasionally.

The strength of the young adult dialogue group is in the wisdom and experiences shared by those present. Once in a while a topic might keep coming up that needs the assistance of an "expert." If the issue of relation-ships is continually raised, the group might invite someone whose work deals with maintaining and assisting healthy human relations. If religious issues keep recurring, the group might invite a religious "expert" to offer insights into the religious questions.

21. Develop trust.

The effectiveness of a dialogue group can be measured by the level of trust. Trust means that people in the group have the freedom to speak and to share, knowing they will be respected and not criticized no matter what they say. Trust implies confidentiality: what is said in the group stays in the group. Trust also means that seemingly foolish things can be said and will not be laughed at or attacked. One sure way to determine whether trust is strong is when an argument occurs. If the issue can be debated, even heatedly, without hurting anyone's feelings, trust is at work. Respect for the individual can be maintained, while disagreement, even heated disagreement, over an issue takes place. If people's feelings are hurt, back off. Trust takes time.

22. Correct behavior as necessary.

The responsibility for correction of behavior rests first with the person who convened the group, second with the leadership that develops, and finally with the whole group. The person who called the group together has the primary responsibility to develop a working relationship among the participants. Correction of behavior can be both positive and negative. It might mean encouraging a person who is shy. It can also mean letting talkative members know that they dominate the discussions and that the group would benefit if they allowed someone else a chance to speak. It can mean asking someone to be less negative or hostile and telling others that their presence is appreciated when it seems they are beginning to doubt their commitment to the group.

23. Don't expect everybody to want to join your group.

A young adult dialogue group is not for everybody. The two criteria for a young adult dialogue group, age and dialogue, will limit participation and membership. For some young adults dialogue is threatening. Some people are just not good at dialogue and do not enjoy it. A young adult dialogue group is not for them. A dialogue group is not just a place to meet people. It has a more specific purpose: conversation and sharing with other young adults about issues and topics of importance. A young adult dialogue group is not for people who do not like groups, who are too shy to speak in public, or who simply are private people.

24. Make time for the unexpected.

As a dialogue group develops and trust among the members is established, there will be times when someone, quite unexpectedly, wishes to share something with the group, seek the wisdom of the group, or seek support on a personal matter. Obviously, that takes precedence over the agenda. Just be careful to be supportive listeners rather than "experts" about a situation you might not fully understand. Often just by verbalizing their concerns, group members can see their situation more clearly. The role of the group is to be supportive.

25. End with dignity.

All good things come to an end. What began with excitement has a right to end with dignity. Try not to let your group end because of attrition, boredom, or frustration. The participants in a young adult group live in a highly mobile, fast-paced world. Needs change. Time commitments vary. Groups should set specific dates for evaluating what is happening, seeing who might need to leave the group, considering whether to add new people, and determining whether the group should continue. We suggest evaluations be held every three months.

Appendix E

Eleven Ways to Use This Retreat Effectively

1. Be still with yourself.

To be still is very difficult, but it can be both important and enjoyable. It takes some work. It means to do nothing. Try to think about nothing. Just breathe. Nothing else. It is difficult because we rarely are still. We live in a world of noise, radios, television, portable stereos, and constant movement. We are always doing something. So much of our life is a task to be accomplished. To be still allows for the possibility of calm to overtake you, a gentleness to happen that helps put life in perspective. If it works for you, then it will remind you that there is more to you than you sense every day. Try it this weekend. Pick a time (no less than a half hour). Pick a place (your room, outside, in the chapel). But don't rush it. Being still with yourself is not another scheduled activity to race through.

2. Take plenty of time for yourself.

To take care of yourself sounds selfish, but it is not necessarily narcissistic. We need to take care of ourselves. So during this weekend retreat figure out what you need to do in your own life, and do it! If you need to rest, nap, relax, read, write, walk, run, sleep longer, pray, then do it. That's what a retreat is all about: retreating from what we do every day to do different and important things.

3. Whatever you have put off, do it.

Often we are so busy that we keep putting things off until later. Let this weekend be that "later." If you have wanted to do something, plan something, think about something, then put it off no longer. Schedule time with yourself this weekend, and keep your appointment!

4. Write things out.

If you attend a conference, take notes during or immediately afterward. Write out some things that struck you. Write out a thought or two that crossed your mind during the presentation. Write out a question or two that occurred to you during the talk. Write yourself a letter. Write out your ideas. Sometimes it's called keeping a journal, your written reflections on the weekend. Put together a written agenda of things you want to accomplish between now and next spring. Who do you owe a letter? Write it.

5. Make a game plan for the weekend.

We have provided you with a schedule for the retreat (conferences, meals, etc.). With that schedule in hand, why not create a personal game plan or schedule? Often if we don't actually schedule things, they will not happen. We've all heard the old saying, "The road to hell is paved with good intentions." Here is a list of some things you might plan this weekend:

...Rest	...Think
...Walk	...Pray
...Wander	...Converse with others
...Exercise	...Be alone
...Read	...Write

Make your schedule now. Establish a few priorities now. Before you know it, it will be Sunday.

6. Do anything you want.

We're adults now, not kids and not teenagers (thank God!). Many young adults have been on retreat only before confirmation, before eighth grade graduation, or during high school. On those retreats everyone did everything together. There was little room for individual decision making. This is a different style of retreat. You are in charge. You can do whatever you wish. If you want to be by yourself and not in a discussion group, then go off and be by yourself. Do what you need to do. Just don't blow the weekend. Time like this is too precious.

7. Attend conferences—if you wish.

The conferences that will take place from Friday night through Sunday morning are to stimulate your thinking, offer insights for your life, and support your faith. Attend them, if you wish. If you would rather skip a conference, that's all right, too. Use these forty hours the best way you can.

8. Schedule individual conferences—if you wish.

Sometimes it's good to talk to someone else. Throughout the weekend you are welcome to ask anyone assisting with the retreat for one-on-one time. Feel free to come and talk about anything going on in your life. Sometimes it is helpful to get an objective opinion or another point of view. Let us know when you would like to meet, and we will do our best to accommodate you.

9. Use small group meetings—if you wish.

Good conversation and sharing are great gifts. During the course of the retreat weekend several opportunities will be offered for you to enter into discussion with others who are here. Through these small groups you will have the opportunity to listen and speak with others, meet new people, listen to new ideas, and share common experiences. If you find small groups helpful, please join one.

10. Don't wait to be told what to do next.

The retreat leaders are not here to entertain you or keep you busy all the time. One of the negative criticisms often heard about this type of retreat is that "they gave us too much free time." Kids are told what to do; adults choose what to do. Kids have to be kept busy all the time; adults choose the level of activity that fits their lifestyle and needs. This is your retreat. Use your time effectively and creatively.

11. Set your agenda on Friday night.

The formal part of our retreat tonight will conclude with a brief time for prayer in the chapel. Afterward, why not take these pages with you? Reread them before you retire for the night, and then make some decisions on what you need to do this weekend. Either before or after breakfast, read over these pages one more time. Finalize your decisions about what you will do on Saturday. A good retreat is well planned.

References

Cusick, John C. "Connecting Collegians." *Church* 6, no. 3 (Fall 1990). *Church* is published by the National Pastoral Life Center, 18 Bleecker St., New York, NY 10012.

Cusick, John C., and Katherine DeVries. "A New Age in the Church: Young Adults." *New Theology Review* (February 1998).

Froehle, Bryan T., and Mary L. Gautier. *Catholicism USA: A Portrait of the Catholic Church in the United States.* New York: Center for Applied Research in the Apostolate, 2000.

National Conference of Catholic Bishops. *Sons and Daughters of the Light: A Pastoral Plan for Ministry with Young Adults.* Washington, D.C.: United States Catholic Conference, 1997.

Sheehy, Gail. *New Passages: Mapping Your Life across Time.* New York: Random House, 1995.

Zullo, James R., F.S.C. *God and Gen-X: Faith and the New Generation.* Romeoville, Ill.: Lewis University Press, 1999.

Index

activities. *See* events; serious activities; service activities; social activities; spiritual activities

advisory board for regional young adult ministry, 92–94

affiliate Catholics
number of, 10
parish pastoral ministers and, 67
practicing Catholics and, 4
ways to deal with, 11

Ainsworth, Elise, 183

Altar and Rosary Society, 30

annulment, 99

Archdiocese of Chicago. *See* Chicago, Archdiocese of

area young adult ministry. *See* regional young adult ministry

associate director of a Young Adult Ministry Office, 112

attendance. *See* Mass

Baby Boomers, 179, 181, 182

baptism
alienation caused by the church's handling of, 11–13
follow-up by parish pastoral ministers after, 67–69
as a moment of return, 66

birth control, 12, 178

bishops, 100, 118–19

brainstorming, 52–53

bulletin announcements, 39–40

campus ministry, 107. *See also* college students

Canon Law, 13

catechesis, 5, 153–56

Catholic culture, 122

Catholicism Revisited Program, 135, 153–55

Catholic student centers, 78

celibacy, 12, 178

census forms, 39

Chancery Office, 99

chaplains, 85

Chicago, Archdiocese of
examples of publicity used by Young Adult Ministry Office of, 133–39
overview of young adult ministry of, xiii–xiv, 108–13, 140–60

college students, 74–79, 107

community newspapers, 40

compassion, 66–67, 120–21

computers, 164. *See also* databases; Internet; web pages; websites

confession, 70

core groups, 55

counselors, 85

databases
diocesan outreach and, 113–15
instructions on building and maintaining, 201–3
regional young adult ministry and, 86, 96

demographics
of adult Catholics, 6
of the U.S. church, 3

dialogue groups, 204–11

dioceses
as advocates for young adult ministry, 100–102
financial commitments of, 107–8
guidelines for event planning in, 125–30
hints for leaders of Young Adult Ministry Offices in, 130–32

217

The Authors

Fr. John Cusick, ordained a priest for the Archdiocese of Chicago, is the director of the Young Adult Ministry Office of the archdiocese. He has been an associate pastor at Mary, Seat of Wisdom Church in Park Ridge, Illinois, and a theology instructor, residence hall director, and director of recruitment and admissions for Niles College Seminary of Loyola University. He resides and assists at Old St. Patrick's Church in downtown Chicago.

Ms. Katherine DeVries, associate director of the Young Adult Ministry Office for the Archdiocese of Chicago, has held that position since 1988. Previously, she was a special education teacher for high school and junior high students with severe behavior disorders and learning disabilities. She holds a master's degree in special education from Northern Illinois University, a master's degree in pastoral studies from Loyola University, and a master of divinity degree with a concentration in Word and Worship from Catholic Theological Union in Chicago. She is an active parishioner at St. Mary's Church in Riverside, Illinois.

Of related interest

Winging It
Meditations of a Young Adult
Therese Johnson Borchard
ISBN 1-57075-357-1, paperback

Honest, enriching reflections for twenty-somethings.

"I highly recommend *Winging It.* It's you. It's life. It's God."
—John Cusick, Director of Young Adult Ministry,
Archdiocese of Chicago

God Moments
Why Faith Really Matters to a New Generation
Jeremy Langford

ISBN 1-57075-390-3, paperback

*A thirty-year-old seeker brings out what is best in Catholicism
as he candidly shares his fascinating spiritual journey.*

"This book is the real thing. Jeremy Langford deftly combines
a variety of genres—personal narrative, theology, and social
commentary—to offer an illuminating look at what it
means to be a seeker in contemporary society."
—James Martin, S.J., author of
This Our Exile and *In Good Company*

Why Not Be a Missioner?
Young Maryknollers Tell Their Stories
Michael Leach and Susan Perry, editors
ISBN 1-57075-391-1, paperback

*Inspiring first-person accounts of young adults
who are serving God and neighbor in every corner of the earth.*

Please support your local bookstore, or call 1-800-258-5838

For a free catalog, please write us at
Orbis Books, Box 308
Maryknoll, NY 10545-0308
or visit our website at www.orbisbooks.com

Thank you for reading *The Basic Guide to Young Adult Ministry.*
We hope you enjoyed it.